Tricked Into Sickness

An Eye-opening Guide to Perfect Health

By

Lola Hardaway

Any healing you have enjoyed, whether physical, mental, emotional, or otherwise which has been administered through a medical doctor, a psychologist, a psychiatrist, a counselor, or even through a supernatural intervention, is only second-rate in comparison to God's desire for total wholeness for all of our lives.

Tricked Into Sickness
An Eye-opening Guide to Perfect Health
1st Edition 2013 © Lola Hardaway and Here's To Your Health

ISBN: 978-0-9899166-0-8

DEDICATION

For making it happen:

First and foremost, I give *TRICKED INTO SICKNESS* back to God through Christ Jesus Who is causing the Holy Spirit to complete the work He has begun regarding this book, for I decree that millions of lives will not only be touched but changed into His image.

Next, I dedicate this work to my precious mother, Rose Hardaway, the channel through whom God has used to funnel His life into me so that this work could be. May you read, record, and receive all that God has prearranged for you through the precious Blood of Jesus. I love you, Mother. Thanks for choosing to live! And, to the priceless memories of my dad, James Hardaway, whose name I have ascribed as author so that it will continue.

To my cousin, Dr. Geneva Moore, the one who is always there to advise me when to stop and when to go, and to add the commas and correct the misplaced modifiers. When this book went to the publisher's editor, the first thing the editor said was, "This book has already been edited." And it was all because of you. Thanks, Gin, for making it easy for all of us. I love you!

I dedicate *TRICKED INTO SICKNESS* to my siblings, Charlene, Cindi, Toot, Kitty, and Luther. May you glean from these words to walk in divine health so that we will all be here when Christ Jesus returns. For your many words of encouragement, thank you! I love you!

Finally, to our great and devoted customers at Here's To Your Health in Jacksonville, Florida, and those we service from afar, thank you for your wonderful support which has come in so many ways and for so many years! You have proven loyal; you have helped to educate us; you have prayed for us; you have laughed with us and even cried with us. You are truly the family of Here's To Your Health. Without you, we would not be here. I love you! May you forever walk in divine health!

And to our readers, HERE'S TO YOUR HEALTH!

TABLE OF CONTENTS

Tricked Into Sickness

INTRODUCTION

As stated by the Physician and Apostle Luke, *"Inasmuch as many have taken in hand to set in order a narrative of those things which have been fulfilled among us, just as those who from the beginning were eyewitnesses and ministers of the word delivered them to us, it seemed good to me also, having had perfect understanding of all things from the very first, to write to you an orderly account, most excellent Theophilus, that you may know the certainty of those things in which you were instructed."*

(Luke 1:1-4 NKJV)

Like the Apostle Luke who was also a physician, I, too, long to impart unto you what God is saying to me through the Holy Spirit as it relates to your health. The Gospels are written of Jesus' earthly journey by four disciples and from four different perspectives or points of view, based on the Holy Spirit's utilization of their fields of expertise: Matthew, a Jew, who reveals prophesies as no other Gospel does; Mark, a Roman warrior, who is the reconnoiterer of the four Gospels, having written the first of these books, writing of the miracles and showing his fearlessness in stepping forth; Dr. Luke, whose expertise is invested in his title, and John who has the revelatory eyes of the heart, having seen Jesus as God.

In the day that the Apostle Matthew wrote his Gospel, he said, *"A wicked and adulterous generation seeks after a sign . . ."* Things have not changed. Today, as never before, and more than anything else

1

in the world, people run to Jesus because they need a healing. Some run to Him because someone very close and dear to them needs immediate restoration. Another reason is that they require a supernatural intervention in their bodies because the doctors have exhausted all measures of treatment and have issued the death sentence. Many are pouring into the Kingdom because they were supernaturally healed, and this is their expression of gratitude. Some have been converted because of miraculous changes in the lives of their loved ones who were touched by the Holy Spirit. A sick body is nothing to celebrate, and it almost always brings much misery into one's life. To say that healing is the children's bread means that God's healing causes the body to be nourished and fully functional. Praise God for the supernatural power of the Holy Ghost! This kind of advertisement cannot be resisted.

I see healing in God's Word from a different point of view. The supernatural healings many of us have received, myself included, are only second-rate to what God wants to do in all of our lives.

My observation on healing has not always been a part of my belief, but neither has any other aspect of my life. Everything changed when I became a born-again Christian. Everything. And that, I believe, is what God wants. *". . . If any man be in Christ, he is a new creature: old things are passed away; behold, all things are become new,"* (2 Corinthians 5:17 KJV). Prior to salvation, I had the mind of Lola, which was the mind of the world. I now have the mind of Christ (1 Corinthians 2:16). I am fully persuaded that what God wrote in His Word is for me. Because I have committed my life to Him, I am who He says I am, and because I have committed my life to Him, I have what He says I have. My identity is not only sealed in Heaven, but it is also sealed in my heart, in my soul, and in my body. In addition, my identity is sealed in the heavenly realm where principalities and powers are placed on notice, and at the mention of the Name of Jesus, they must bow.

During my years as a convert, God opened my eyes and caused me to understand the role that "sick demons" (You may call them "spirits of infirmity".) play in the spirit realm. Please be open to view life from a different perspective. Some of what you read here has been told before, but not by me. You see, *"That which is being told has already been, and what has been will be already done, for there is nothing new under the sun,"* (Ecclesiastes 1:9 NKV). It is my aim to present these revelations to you in a manner which makes God's truths irresistible.

The Holy Bible is an antiquity of the antiquities, yet, no word in it has changed. More books are written *about* the Holy Bible than any other book in the entire world. People are so fascinated, engulfed, entrenched, intrigued, enlightened, excited, curious, or enraged, infuriated, and insulted… the list could go on into eternity, so they simply want to share their personal little revelation, or opinion, or disagreement with the world about an infallible, undisputable, incorruptible Word. Clap, clap to some; shame, shame to others. And yet, of all the millions of books written about the Bible, there is none which has outsold the Holy Scriptures. Even today, it sells at a rate of 23,000,000, annually. How beautiful it is to know that the very first book ever to be printed on the newly invented Gutenberg printing press was a Latin edition of the Holy Scriptures in the year 1450.

> *"My doctrine shall drop as the rain, my speech shall distil as the dew, as the small rain upon the tender herb, and as the showers upon the grass: Because I will publish the name of the Lord: ascribe ye greatness unto our God. He is the Rock, his work is perfect: for all his ways are judgment: a God of truth and without iniquity, just and right is he."*
> (Deuteronomy 32:2-4 KJV)

"The Lord gave the Word: great was the company of those that published it," (Psalms 68:11). It is my prayer that God will direct

this book to those who need it most, and that they will apply these Biblical principles so that they, too, will enjoy the benefits of 3 John 2:

> *"Beloved, I wish above all things that thou mayest prosper and be in health, even as thy soul prospereth."*
>
> (3 John 1:2)

And just as I have had an awakening regarding healing as it relates to God's Promises, it is also my prayer that you are able to glean from my experiences and enjoy the healthy life I am enjoying simply by taking God at His Word. I am a fanatic for believing that God meant exactly what He wrote. I pray that you will be, too, once you have opened your heart and permitted the entrance of His Word to give you light.

> *"The entrance of Your words gives light, it gives understanding to the simple."*
>
> (Psalm 119:130 NKJV)

> *"Finally, brethren, pray for us, that the word of the Lord may run swiftly and be glorified, just as it is with you, and that we may be delivered from unreasonable and wicked men, for not all have faith."*
>
> (2 Thessalonians 3:1-2 NKJV)

Because some will even reject knowledge, God has no choice but to reject them.

> *"My people are ruined because they don't know what's right or true. Because you've turned your back on knowledge, I've turned my back on you priests [those who are in God's Kingdom]. Because you refuse to recognize the revelation of God . . ."*
>
> (Hosea 4:6 MSG)

But, to those who have faith to believe, receive, and act on God's powerful, infallible, inerrant, incorruptible Word, I say, "Here's To Your Health."

Chapter One

FOOD: FRIEND OR FOE

"He causes the grass to grow for the cattle, And vegetation for the service of man, So that he may bring forth food from the earth."

(Psalm 104:14 NKJV)

C hief demon satan doesn't have any new tricks, just new people. Food can be either your best friend or your worst enemy, depending on what you eat and how it's prepared or processed. Oftentimes, during work hours, we have so much fun exchanging health information with many of our knowledgeable customers, especially customers such as Gary Christopher who was diagnosed with terminal cancer. ("Terminal", incidentally, means fatal, and Gary literally shocked the medical staff at one local hospital when his so-called "terminal" cancer all but disappeared after following a strict alternative health regimen.) During one of our fun times, Gary said, "We've got to eat from the farm and not the factory." Eating from the farm is what brings life, so it would behoove those of us who can plant a garden to do exactly that. Whatever you decide to place in your mouth to consume for health and nourishment, simply remember that you cannot improve upon God's wholesome foods coming straight from the earth.

WHATEVER YOU PLACE IN YOUR MOUTH TO CONSUME FOR HEALTH AND NOURISHMENT, KNOW THAT YOU CANNOT IMPROVE ON GOD'S NATURAL FOODS COMING STRAIGHT FROM THE EARTH

Food is the first provision God created for the sustenance of man, after He created a conducive living environment: *"Then God said, 'Let the earth bring forth grass, the herb that yields seed, and the fruit tree that yields fruit according to its kind, whose seed is in itself, on the earth,' "* (Genesis 1:11). A perfect and upright God would not have dared place His children in a world where the ground was infertile, barren, and ill-equipped to sustain them in their original state of Creation. When we compare God's first five days of Creation (the heavens and the Earth, the sun, moon and stars, the waters and the seas, the animals and winged fowls and the birds and fishes, etc.), which He saw was "good" with His highest form of Creation (man and woman) whom He made in His image and in His likeness, which He saw was "very good", we must be at ease in knowing that our "excellent" God would create nothing less than healing foodstuff to maintain His immortal Creation — immortal, that is, before man's fall. God's initial intent was never to have His family separated from Himself, and certainly not because of sickness or death. As an example for every good father, before bringing His children to Himself, God made every provision for them to live wholesomely and to exist in the opulence of His Creation. When He brought them forth from the power of His Spirit, He blessed them first, no doubt with wisdom to obey His instructions, knowing that He had given them the "will to choose." After blessing them, He instructed them: *"Be fruitful and multiply; fill the earth and subdue it; have dominion over the fish of the sea, over the birds of the air, and over every living thing that moves on the earth . . . See, I have given you every herb that yields seed which is on the face of all the earth, and every tree whose fruit yields seed; to you it shall be for food."* (Genesis 1:28-29)

We see here that from the beginning of Creation, FOOD was God's antidote for maintaining man's body and soul. Not just any food, but the "living food" that grows and moves on the Earth . . . unprocessed food . . . food that has life in itself. This was God's original intent for our nourishment, and it remains His intent today. *"For I am the LORD, I change not . . ."* (Malachi 3:6 KJV). "Excellent" is always greater than "very good", so remember that the ways of an excellent God are always higher than those of His Creation, and you cannot improve upon God. Food in its original and rawest form is God's original plan for our sustenance.

> *"And by the river upon the bank thereof, on this side and on that side, shall grow all trees for meat, whose leaf shall not fade, neither shall the fruit thereof be consumed: it shall bring forth new fruit according to his months, because their waters they issued out of the sanctuary: and the fruit thereof [from the trees] shall be for meat [food], and the leaf thereof [from the trees] for medicine [for your health and healing]."*
>
> (Ezekiel 47:12 KJV, notes added)

The Trick Began in the Garden of Eden out of satan's* Jealousy and Humankind's Disobedience

(*I have chosen to adopt T. D. Jake's position and not capitalize the "s" in satan out of lack of respect for him.)

When giving instructions to Adam to have dominion over all the Earth, God explained to him that the trees allocated for him and his offspring were those growing on both sides of the riverbanks. These trees would bear fruit (food) incessantly so that they would never hunger. The leaves of these trees were to be eaten as medicine so that they would forever walk in divine health.

Chief demon satan was once Heaven's most beautiful and talented angel of all, and he had held a place of great esteem and authority while residing there. He was the overseer of praise and worship — the most secure job ever assigned — because just as there will be no end to God's government (Isaiah 9:7), His

7

praises will ring throughout eternity. God wants us to praise Him, forever:

"To the end that my glory may sing praise to You and not be silent. O LORD my God, I will give thanks to You forever."
(Psalm 30:12 NKJV)

"I will praise You, O Lord my God, with all my heart. And I will glorify Your Name forevermore."
(Psalm 86:12 NKJV)

Moreover, the only reason God created humankind was for us to worship Him. In Exodus 8 (NIV), God told Moses to go and tell Pharaoh to let His people go, *"So that they may worship me."*

Think about it: What can we possibly do for God except to worship and praise Him? One may say that he is on an assignment for God, which demands physical and mental work. However, the end result of that task will generally bring great gain to the individual, and because of the success, God gets the glory. Thus, the work is done through us, but the praise and worship is given to God for causing us to succeed. So you see, the appointment given to Lucifer during his tenure in Heaven was both prestigious and enormous, for the praises of God's people toward Him never cease.

When we were children and we were disobedient, my mother would say, "I'm giving you just enough rope to hang yourself." Today, I understand that phrase: God allowed Lucifer to lead the heavenly choir. Lucifer's leadership role, I repeat, was major because I understand that in Heaven thousands upon thousands of songs are being sung at one time, and although the songs ring out in harmony, you can distinctly hear the words and melody of each one, singularly and with precision. Conducting that kind of choir takes a major skill which can only be accomplished through God and in Heaven, and such a meticulous task was assigned to Lucifer. But how arrogant of Lucifer to think that he, alone, was performing such a skill all on his own! Lucifer was an angel, and angels are sent to help or service those who are to receive salvation, not to rule over them.

> *"But to which of the angels said he at any time, Sit on my right hand, until I make thine enemies thy footstool? Are they not all ministering spirits, sent forth to minister for them who shall be heirs of salvation?"*
> (Hebrews 1:13-14 KJV)

The role got to be too much for Lucifer because he could not handle the accolades. Things got out of hand when he wanted to take over:

> *"For thou hast said in thine heart, I will ascend into heaven, I will exalt my throne above the stars of God: I will sit also upon the mount of the congregation, in the sides of the north: I will ascend above the heights of the clouds; I will be like the most High."*
> (Isaiah 14:13-14 KJV)

God has made it clear that He is the Creator of all Creation. Heaven belongs to Him, and He makes no bones about it:

> *"Heaven is my throne and earth is my footstool . . ."*
> (Isaiah 66:1 NKJV)

> *"Behold, the heaven and the heaven of heavens is the LORD's thy God, the earth also, with all that therein is."*
> (Deuteronomy 10:14 KJV)

> *"Thine, O LORD is the greatness, and the power, and the glory, and the victory, and the majesty; for all that is in the heaven and in the earth is thine; thine is the kingdom, O LORD, and thou art exalted as head above all."*
> (1 Chronicles 29:11 KJV)

Mind you, God knows your thoughts before you are able to act upon them:

> *"O LORD, You have searched me and known me. You know my sitting down and my rising up; You understand my thought afar off."*
>
> (Psalm 139:1-2 NKJV)

He caught the stench of pride, arrogance, and "entertainment" in the haughty spirit of Choir Conductor, Lucifer, as opposed to his worshiping Him in spirit and in truth, for *"God is Spirit, and those who worship Him must worship [Him] in spirit and truth,"* (John 4:24 NKJV, note added). Not so in Heaven. Lucifer had to go! Not only did Lucifer have to go, but so did all of the angels who had taken their eyes off the Most High God and had begun moving into Lucifer's jam session. Yes, sir, they had to vacate the premises, too.

> *"Thy pomp is brought down to the grave, and the noise of thy viols: the worm is spread under thee, and the worms cover thee. How art thou fallen from heaven, O Lucifer, son of the morning! how art thou cut down to the ground, which didst weaken the nations! Yet thou shalt be brought down to hell, to the sides of the pit. They that see thee shall narrowly look upon thee, and consider thee, saying, Is this the man that made the earth to tremble, that did shake kingdoms."*
>
> (Isaiah 14:11-16 KJV)

God, the Supreme Creator of the heavens and the Earth and all that they contain, will not give His glory to another.

> *"I am the LORD: that is my name: and my glory will I not give to another, neither my praise to graven images."*
>
> (Isaiah 42:8 KJV)

He kicked satan out of Heaven like a bolt of lightening! Lucifer had been over the heavenly choir and during his tenure, he sought to undermine God by placing himself as Heaven's leader. God had given him this colossal assignment, and he took it upon himself to give himself a promotion, forgetting that, *"Promotion comes neither from the east, nor from the west, nor from the south. But God is the judge: he putteth down one, and setteth up another,"* (Psalm 75:6-7 KJV). Lucifer had to go!

God never gave satan a mind and abilities comparable to His. When God created humanity, satan saw that He had created a replica of Himself — the exact position he tried to seize while in heaven — and he became enraged. If you have lived any length of time, at least once in your life, you have heard of a person becoming so blazingly jealous that he or she committed murder. It is this same demonic spirit that caused Cain to kill his brother Abel. Abel was obedient in presenting to God his first and perfect lamb as a sacrificial offering, while Cain simply gave God some of his crop, probably the leftovers. God is no respecter of persons, but He is a respecter of hearts toward Him. Abel's heart was pure, and his love for God demanded that he give God nothing less than his very best. Cain, on the other hand, was selfish, and he kept his best crop for himself and gave God something for a show. When God saw that Cain's offering was not a willing sacrifice, He did not accept it. God had graciously received Abel's unselfish forthright offering, and this made Cain uncontrollably angry. That's when the murder-demon took control. This demonic spirit was initiated when satan first saw Adam's father/ child relationship with God and how generous God was to His children. He overheard some of the daily conversations Adam and God had, and he even reflected on his assignment in Heaven where he thought, at the time, that he had been given the greatest power next to God Himself. He was wrong. God had given Adam complete control over all the Earth. Not only had God given man the Earth, but He also created him with organs to reproduce after God's kind and to fill the entire Earth with little gods.

> *"Jesus answered them, Is it not written in your law, I said, Ye are gods?"*
>
> (John 10:34 KJV)

> *"I have said, Ye are gods; and all of you are children of the most High."*
>
> (Psalm 82:6 KJV)

No one had ever imagined such power — these little gods would all be running the entire world!

> *"And God blessed them, and God said unto them, Be fruitful, and multiply, and replenish the earth, and subdue it: and have dominion over the fish of the sea, and over the fowl of the air, and over every living thing that moveth upon the earth."*
>
> (Genesis 1:28 KJV)

Demon-satan wasn't about to stand for that. He had to do something to gain control, so he devised a plan. The plan? Kill, steal, and destroy (see John 10:10): kill man, steal the Earth, and destroy God's plan for man's eternal life.

> *"The LORD God took the man and put him in the Garden of Eden to work it and take care of it. And the LORD God commanded the man, 'You are free to eat from any tree in the garden; but you must not eat from the tree of the knowledge of good and evil, for when you eat of it you will surely die.' "*
>
> (Genesis 2:15-16 NIV)

Demon-satan had to find the best and most effective way to accomplish his goal, and that would be to trick man out of the very thing that God had given him which would enable him to enjoy eternal life.

"Now the serpent was more crafty than any of the wild animals the LORD God had made. He said to the woman, 'Did God really say, "You must not eat from any tree in the garden"?' The woman said to the serpent, 'We may eat fruit from the trees in the garden, but God did say, "You must not eat fruit from the tree that is in the middle of the garden, and you must not touch it, or you will die.' " 'You will not surely die,' the serpent said to the woman. 'For God knows that when you eat of it your eyes will be opened, and you will be like God, knowing good and evil.' And when the woman saw that the tree was good for food, and that it was pleasant to the eyes, and a tree to be desired to make one wise, she took of the fruit thereof, and did eat, and gave also unto her husband with her, and he did eat. And the eyes of them both were opened, and they knew that they were naked; and they sewed fig leaves together, and made themselves aprons."
(Genesis 3:1-7 NIV)

Thus, God's original plan for man to live eternally and in divine health was terminated by the disobedience of Adam and Eve. Notice, satan operates through the "power of suggestion". He had no power to terminate the Edenic Covenant, but he was persuasive enough to convince Eve to eat from the forbidden Tree of Knowledge of Good and Evil. Eve, in turn, convinced her husband, and the entire human race fell into sin, with Adam being its father, but satan being its author. Man could no longer enjoy his supper from the Garden of Eden because the gates were now closed. Sin always shuts us off from God's presence. Instead of man reaching up to the trees to gather his food, he now had to stoop down and work for it by plowing through thorns and thistles from the fields, harvesting his own crops. Because it was "food" that brought sin into the world, God now cursed the ground, which produced the food, by forcing man to work by the sweat of his brow in order to eat. God, in His infinite mercy and His unparalleled love for man, did not curse the food but only the ground, causing man to pay for his disobedience. (If it wasn't for Heaven's strict rules of forgiving and forgetting, most of us would search for Adam and Eve when we got there and take this matter up with them.) Isn't it wonderful that we are not God? Can you imagine how Adam must have felt when he tilled the ground? Every few feet there would crawl a snake on its belly to remind him of how foolishly he had behaved when he disobeyed God by listening to his wife. The death penalty was now implemented. In addition to the hard work, man would contract sicknesses and would die. The entire human race was tricked out of eternal life and into sickness.

Chapter Two

FIRST THINGS FIRST . . .
How Long Will You Toddle?

"Then we will no longer be infants, tossed back and forth by the waves, and blown here and there by every wind of teaching and by the cunning and craftiness of men in their deceitful scheming. Instead, speaking the truth in love, we will in all things grow up into him who is the Head, that is, Christ. From him the whole body, joined and held together by every supporting ligament, grows and builds itself up in love, as each part does its work."

(Ephesians 4:14-16 NIV)

Stagnated Christians are deprived, underprivileged, undernourished, spiritually bankrupt, and mentally impoverished Christians. Oh, and they are physically misled, too. They are Christians who learn scripture, quote scripture, even enjoy scripture, frequently visit the holy edifice, and often play a role in church activities. Many sing in the choir, work with the Usher Board, or work in some other church auxiliary, but their lives reveal as much carnality as a person who has not surrendered his or her life to Christ Jesus, i.e., a sinner. You cannot distinguish most stagnated Christians from the world, because they continue to conduct their lives by feelings rather than by faith.

". . . the flesh profiteth nothing . . ."

(John 6:63 KJV)

Whether it is a symptom of sickness or a signal of economic cataclysm, a staggering Christian will snatch hold of the feeling or farce and plant himself right in the middle.

Case and point: My precious mother is eighty-nine years of age, and I delight in the spiritual improvement she has made since she has begun studying God's Word. But two or three years is a very short time to undo eighty-plus years of habitual practice. A year or so ago, my mother began complaining about her eyesight. "My vision is getting worse and worse," she would say each time she held the glasses to her eyes. "I've got to go to the eye doctor and get stronger glasses." Each time she spoke those words, I gingerly tried to correct her by quoting God's Word, but she was determined that her vision was worsening, so I resolved to lead by example. In my attempts to help her redirect her thoughts, she rebelled, "You can't tell me what I'm seeing!"

I chose a different approach by using myself as an example, "Well, Mother, I thank God that my vision is getting better and better." Wouldn't you know it? When my mother went to have her eyes checked, she was prescribed stronger lenses. In fact, I had been able to see out of her old glasses, but the new ones were too strong for me. I wear glasses, too. My last trip to the ophthalmologist sent me running to the mass-market for eyeglasses when I witnessed the doctor take my commercial glasses, read the Rx, and write me a $400.00 prescription based on the reading from the commercial lenses. I have been purchasing commercial glasses ever since, and until last year, the strength was +125. Now, after the battle of the eyeballs with my mother, my vision has improved, and the prescription has weakened to +100. I chose to speak life into my vision, and God honored my words.

One of the all-encompassing, ever-compelling Scriptures I learned as a new Christian was:

"For assuredly, I say to you, whoever says to this mountain, 'Be removed and be cast into the sea,' and does not doubt in his heart, but believes that those things he says will be done, he will have whatever he says."

(Mark 11:23 NKJV)

The word "say" within Jesus' teaching is used three (3) times. Jesus is instructing His disciples to speak out or call out any situation or thing that their hearts may desire. Then, He goes a step further by telling them to command the thing to exist and affirm its existence at the time they are commanding it to come forth. Within the same context, however, Jesus admonishes His disciples not to allow doubt to enter into their hearts. Notice, Jesus did not say, "and does not doubt in his 'head'," but *"and does not doubt in his 'heart'."* Not doubting with his "heart" simply means not doubting what God has written in His Word. Remember, satan can only introduce thoughts or ideas to your "mind". It is up to you to either accept the devil's thoughts or to reject them.

Another great example which you may recall is the anticipation of Y2K (incoming of the year 2000). Beginning in 1996, predictions ranging from the apocalypse to an international computer bug destroying our world economy tormented the entire world. Merchants enjoyed a gold rush, earning trillions of dollars to accommodate the fears of the world. People stashed away food to last for years. They purchased thermal clothing to support inclement weather conditions; generators were purchased in the event there was an electrical outage; underground shelters were built in homes where they could afford it; many drew their savings from banks, and the list goes on. And what happened? Absolutely nothing.

A Christian who does not make a concerted effort to read, study, and rehearse the Word of God both mentally and orally on a daily basis cannot be a disciple of God, because he or she will never have a transformed mind. I've seen some very academically accomplished, intellectually stimulating Christians who can't seem to make it from point A to point B without intense struggle and drama in their lives surrounding the most elementary events. The reason is that these folks believe that 'church has its place', and they have far removed themselves from the true church, which is the Body of Christ — *Christ in us, the hope of glory.* Although many have confessed Christ as their Savior, they have not transformed their minds to realize that true Christianity is based on trusting and not feeling, and on giving and not taking.

> *"He shall not be afraid of evil tidings: his heart is fixed, trusting in the LORD."*
>
> (Psalm 112:7 KJV)

And:

> *"Charity suffered long, and is kind; charity envieth not; charity vaunted not itself; is not puffed up. Doth not behave itself unseemly, seeketh not her own, is not easily provoked, thinketh no evil; Rejoiceth not in iniquity, but rejoiceth in the truth; 'Beareth all things, believeth all things, hopeth all things, endureth all things.' "*
>
> (1 Corinthians 4:4-7 KJV)

When it comes to tackling what carnal Christians address as "the real world matters", they conclude that their situations must be handled the way the world handles them. How often do we hear "Christians" say, "I know what the Bible says, but I'm dealing with the 'real world' or 'I'm dealing with the facts.' "? This is an assault on the entire Christian family as well as an affront to God!

Love is both the link and the axe that molds and grinds a Christian into the image of Christ Jesus. At the time of salvation, *". . . the love of God is shed abroad in our hearts by the Holy Ghost*

18

which is given unto us," (Romans 5:5 KJV). We now become bound to Christ Jesus: He in us, and we in Him, just as He prayed to the Father:

> *"As thou hast sent me into the world, even so have I also sent them into the world. And for their sakes I sanctify myself, that they also might be sanctified through the truth. Neither pray I for these alone, but for them also which shall believe on me through their word; That they all may be one; as thou, Father, art in me, and I in thee, that they also may be one in us: that the world may believe that thou hast sent me. And the glory which thou gavest me I have given them; that they may be one, even as we are one: I in them, and thou in me, that they may be made perfect in one; and that the world may know that thou hast sent me, and hast loved them, as thou hast loved me."*
>
> (John 17:18-23 KJV)

LOVE IS BOTH THE LINK AND THE AXE THAT MOLDS AND GRINDS A CHRISTIAN INTO THE IMAGE OF CHRIST JESUS

The capacity for each born-again Christian to operate in agape love — an unqualified, unreserved, unconditional, unrestrictive, God-type love, is infused into our spirits the very moment the Holy Spirit comes into our hearts to bring us eternal life, which is the God-life in us. Now it is up to us. Where do we begin? ". . . *Speaking the truth in love, we will in all things grow up into him who is the Head, that is, Christ."* It all begins with our mouths. Purpose in your heart that you will speak only the truth, and the truth is God's Word. Remember, truth is not fact.

The Difference Between "Truth" and "Fact"

Facts are pieces of information, based on scientific studies which can be measured. Not only can facts be measured, but also with the increase of knowledge on an ongoing basis, it is found that facts which are presented in textbooks are outdated within two or three decades. Thus, a matter once called *"fact"* cannot be defined as such, if it is superseded by changing studies. Biology, as a historical science, is a perfect example. Knowledge in the study of biology is changing constantly, and the new information discovered invalidates and abandons the old. Once the old information has been refuted, it is no longer factual. Ironically, what was once a "fact" now becomes a falsehood — the complete opposite of truth. A perfect example is the discovery of DNA. Donald Riley, PhD of the University of Washington, posts his explanation and calls it "DNA EXPLAINED IN EASY TERMS":

> "DNA is material that governs inheritance of eye color, hair color, stature, bone density, and many other human and animal traits. DNA is a long, but narrow string-like object. A one-foot long string or strand of DNA is normally packed into a space roughly equal to a cube 1/millionth of an inch on a side. This is possible only because DNA is a very thin string.
>
> Our body's cells each contain a complete sample of our DNA. One cell is roughly equal in size to the cube described in the previous paragraph. There are muscle cells, brain cells, liver cells, blood cells, sperm cells, and others. Basically, every part of the body is made up of these tiny cells and each contains a sample or complement of DNA identical to that of every other cell within a given person. There are a few exceptions. For example,

our red blood cells lack DNA. Blood itself can be
typed because of the DNA contained in our white
blood cells."

Without explaining in graphic details, let us take a look at
two specific criminal cases. Of course, there have been many
other cases, but for the sake of illustrating my point, we will only
focus on these:

(1) See www.beyondintractability.org: Kirk Noble Bloodsworth,
a commercial fisherman from Maryland, was convicted for the
rape and murder of a nine-year-old girl named Dawn Hamilton
in 1984. Bloodsworth was convicted on the counts that he was
seen leaving the woods around the time the murder occurred,
and his description matched the description of the suspect. An
act strongly staged against him was the "fact" that he tried to
leave the county soon after the crime was revealed. All the while,
Bloodsworth insisted that he was innocent and that he had never
before seen the child. Bloodsworth spent nine years in jail, two of
which were spent as a death-row inmate.

(2) Gary Dotson: In 1979, Gary Dotson was convicted in Chicago
for raping 16-year-old Cathleen Crowell. According to Crowell's
testimony — statements that the criminal court system labeled as
"facts" — Dotson was one of three young men who chased after
her and raped her. She picked Dotson from a book of mug shots
that the police showed her because his face matched the composite
sketch the police made out of her story. As a result, Dotson was
convicted and sentenced to 25 to 50 years in jail for his crime. In
1988, DNA testing proved that the semen stain found on Crowell's
body belonged to her boyfriend, and Dotson was set free.

These two heinous cases occurred prior to the discovery of
DNA and resulted in two innocent men being accused of rape
or murder. Both men served jail time. The courts based their
decisions on the "facts" presented. Moreover, the discovery

of DNA forensics in 1985 has contradicted what was once "facts" and proved the innocence of both of these men based on "truth". "Truth" unlike "facts" will never alter, nor can it be altered.

The simplest definition for DNA, which I found in www. biology4kids, states that "DNA stands for Deoxyribonucleic acid, and it is in the nucleus of a cell and contains all the genetic information of the cell. DNA is a double helix structure where doctors can look at a person's genome (all the DNA in a human) and prevent any genetic disorder like Trisomy 21 and Turner syndrome."

Since DNA is tested from an untampered part of human composition, it is clear that it cannot be changed. As such, test results from DNA make the findings "true" or "truthful". Since its discovery in 1985, DNA testing has revolutionized the way forensic science does its job. People previously convicted of heinous crimes are now being set free because of new DNA evidence proving them to be innocent of the crimes they were accused of in the first place. Prior to DNA testing having become the standard in forensic science, law enforcers, and prosecutors classified eyewitness testimonies, lie detector tests, confessions, and even circumstantial evidence as "facts". Today, however, there are so many cases once considered "fact" that have been reclassified, ultimately nullifying those "fact" findings. Anything that changes cannot be considered "truth", and when "fact" changes, whether past, present, or future, it should never be considered as "truth".

Truth cannot be measured, and truth will never change. The word "truth" has been theorized in countless studies with countless conclusions. However, as Christians, we needn't speculate or theorize. Our unchanging triune God — God the Father, God the Son, God the Holy Spirit — is the all-inclusive definition of "truth". (See John 14:6)

Perfect examples of "truth" are found from the beginning of Creation throughout the Holy Scriptures. God has explicitly given us His Word, and He has clearly spelled out what we can expect when obeying it. Consider the following: A medical report indicates that a person has cancer, or multiple sclerosis, or lupus, or some other debilitating disease, and the doctor conveys the results of these tests plus a prognosis, which is his or her opinion. The doctor's conclusions are based on medical facts taken from years of laboratory studies and probably similar case studies he or she has treated. Honor the doctors, for they are passing on what they have been taught. Thank God they are able to give prognoses, projections, and express professional points of view.

However, as a practicing Christian, your spirit is probably grieved after hearing such a report, and all you are able to witness is the inner voice screaming, "Reject! Reject! Reject!" The Word in you becomes alive, and you have a different point of view. You are a Christian who operates only by Kingdom principles, and according to the head physician from your country, the diagnosis reads that you have been made whole.

> *"Now therefore ye are no more strangers and foreigners, but fellow citizens with the saints, and of the household of God."*
>
> (Ephesians 2:19)

> *"But He was wounded for our transgressions, He was bruised for our iniquities; The chastisement for our peace was upon Him, And by His stripes we are healed."*
>
> (Isaiah 53:5 NKJV)

> *"And he said unto him, Arise, go thy way: thy faith hath made thee whole."*
>
> (Luke 17:19 KJV)

Are you able to recall from experience or studies how deadly pneumonia once was? Since scientist and Doctor Hippocrates, the father of medicine, discovered the deadly disease of pneumonia, the disease has been observed in so many forms that scientists have broken it down into categories. Just to name a few, fungal pneumonia, viral pneumonia, atypical pneumonia, community pneumonia, ventilator-associated pneumonia, and hospital-acquired pneumonia are all included in this long list. The latter two, ventilator-associated and hospital-acquired pneumonia are so common in hospitalized patients that scientists have given them a specific category. This tells us that it comes as no surprise to doctors and hospital personnel when a patient contracts pneumonia while being treated in a hospital environment and while using a ventilator.

www.CNN.com February 23, 2010 *CNN Medical News Managing Editor By Miriam Falco:*

"Researchers believe 48,000 deaths could have been prevented and $8.1 billion dollars saved in the United States, if patients had not gotten infections after being admitted to a hospital. Previous research has shown an association between deaths and hospital infections, but according to a new study, it's difficult to figure out whether the patient actually got the infection in the hospital.

In the study, published in the Archives of Internal Medicine, the authors set out to find out how many patients died because they were infected in the hospital.

Just the way we know that there are 15,000 people who die every year in this country because of HIV, we should know how many people die because of infections they got in the hospital," says Ramanan Laxminarayan, a senior fellow at the social sciences think tank Resources for the Future. He and his colleagues wanted to find out how many people became sickened by pneumonia or sepsis (a life-threatening infection that had spread throughout the body) while they were hospitalized. They looked at 69 million hospital discharge records from 40 states between 1998 and 2006. In an effort to rule out patients that already had infections or were so sick they would not have survived even without a hospital-acquired infection, researchers considered only patients who went in for elective surgery, not because of an emergency.

These were people that the surgeon would not have operated on if they showed any signs of infection and not being well," Laxminarayan explains. He says that judging by the number of patients who then got an infection as opposed to those who didn't, there were an estimated 290,000 cases of hospital-acquired sepsis and 200,000 cases of hospital-acquired pneumonia in 2006. Further, he said, "48,000 sepsis and pneumonia deaths can be attributed to hospital-acquired infections every year."

In addition to the loss of life, these infections add to health care cost. The researchers estimate that the extra hospital days lead to $8.1 billion in added cost."

From the Archives of Internal Medicine: "This count includes only those cases reported. It would be wonderful if there was a health advocate group who made accessible to the public a system for counting where anyone contracting pneumonia while in the hospital would push a button so that their name could be added to the list. . ."

Fast forward five or six decades, and what do we have? Today, a case of pneumonia should no longer be a threat, especially when the main contributors for a solution may be as simple as colloidal silver and high doses of vitamin C to help heal the lungs and build a strong immune system, which Dr. Phyllis Balch writes in her book *Prescription for Nutritional Healing*.

Conclusion: Fact found fatal.

A very important point: When we operate in truth, we must adopt the whole truth, and that includes adopting God's dietary principles. I highly recommend that you invest in Dr. Don Colbert's book *What Would Jesus Eat.* According to Dr. Colbert, when writing advice for his audience and patients to follow, he said, "I thought I'd go back to the training manual — the Bible — and see what Jesus ate. Lo and behold, Jesus ate the healthiest diet ever developed, the Mediterranean diet." If you know anything about the Mediterranean diet, it is claimed to be among the healthiest diet created.

Some of Dr. Colbert's main suggestions for incorporating a healthy Mediterranean health style (short version):

1. Eliminate all processed food and hydrogenated fats.
2. Cook and bake with whole-grain products. Eat more fresh fruits and vegetables, beans, legumes, and nuts.
3. Substitute olive oil for butter, margarine, salad dressings, and other oils. No fried food.
4. Limit cheese intake.
5. Eat low-fat plain yogurt, add fruit, sweeten with Stevia.
6. Choose fish and poultry over red meats.
7. No sugary sweets.
8. Exercise, enjoy friends and family, and I add, read Bible daily.

(Dr. Colbert included one glass of wine daily, but since I am not a wine drinker, I use grape seed extract or Pycnogenol.)

Epidemiological studies reveal that Mediterraneans suffer less heart disease than northern Europeans, and nutritionists observe that the diet reduces fat and increases natural occurring antioxidants, which is attributed to reducing the risk of heart attacks. (See http://www.answers.com/topic/mediterranean-diet#ixzz1D3jaIZlv)

Truth, my beloved, will stand when all else fails. I believe that being truthful is one of the most powerful characteristics one can have. During an assembly at Crenshaw Christian Center, I heard Dr. Frederick Price boldly proclaim that he did not lie. I had never heard anyone make such a profound statement before. Prior to that meeting, but after I was born again, I certainly did not make a practice of lying, but it never occurred to me about the seriousness of the little white lies most people, including myself, told. I have even heard them addressed as "innocent lies" or "harmless lies". When Dr. Price made that bold statement, it ignited something in me that has set a flame up until this very day. I get a joy out of knowing that I don't have to lie. The one thing those who know me closely will say is that if Lola says it, it's true. Under the pretense of "innocence", the devil has tricked most saints into believing that it is all right to tell these little lies. These little so-called "guiltless, no-harm lies" are the primary cause for the downfall of the saints. Many of us have never been taught that we have the ability to speak the truth at all times, and these lies keep us from triumphing. It is the little foxes that spoil the vine (Song of Solomon 2:15). These baby foxes find the grape vines and gnaw away at the base of them, stem by stem, bit by bit, until all of the grapes are dead. Each little so-called, no-harm lie represents one of those little foxes. When a lie is told, it triggers a signal. This is how satan tricks the saints of God into thinking that the sap from the vine is still flowing through their spiritual life when it has been cut off. Every little white lie sends a deadly volt through the nerve sheaths of the body, triggering more and more harm to the body. This is exactly how satan tricks the saints of God from walking in divine health, abundant wealth, peace that passes understanding, i.e., prosperity. He simply tricks us into thinking that we are unable to speak the truth at all times. Moreover, truth is a weapon! When it comes to defeating the devil, truth is one of our main lines of defense.

> *"Wherefore take unto you the whole armor of God, that ye may be able to withstand in the evil day, and having done all, to stand. Stand therefore, having your loins girt about with truth, and having on the breastplate of righteousness."*
>
> (Ephesians 6:12-13 KJV)

Purpose in your heart that the words you speak will always be true, and they will be spoken in love, not tearing down, but building up. Your words will either heal or kill.

> *"[The Lord] satisfies your mouth with good things so that your youth [and strength] is renewed like the eagle's."*
>
> (Psalms 103:5 NKJV, notes added)

So you see, your mouth is very much a determining factor in the status of your health. Speaking the truth in love will cause us to grow more and more like Christ, as the Scripture points out, and I am most certain that Christ was not infirmed. *Ephesians 4:16* indicates that in Christ the whole body, joined and held together by every supporting ligament, grows and builds itself up in love, as each part does its work. We are in Christ and Christ is in God. When we speak the truth in love, we are speaking Christ. We are speaking God because God is love, and Jesus is the truth. So here we are, with love and truth abiding in us, and love and truth are emitted from us. As such, we are knitting, binding, and welding the whole body together, tissue by tissue, bone by bone, joint by joint, binding and sealing, until we become one. As Christ is one with the Father, so are we one with Him. You with me, and I with you. Just as it is in any other skilled profession, we must develop both truth and love to bring it to a place of perfection and to bring us to the place of oneness. Our practicing the constant presence of God, speaking only truth, speaking only love, joining forces to become co-laborers with Him, hooking up with him or linking with Him on a moment-by-moment basis, helps us to grow up and reach maturity.

And, while we are linking forces with the Holy Spirit, we are also cutting off all of the old man. *"Knowing this, that our old man is crucified with him, that the body of sin might be destroyed, that henceforth we should not serve sin. For he that is dead is freed from sin. Do not lie to one another, since you have put off the old man with his deeds,"* (Colossians 3:9). *"And so I insist — and God backs me up on this — that there be no going along with the crowd, the empty-headed, mindless crowd. They've refused for so long to deal with God that they've lost touch not only with God but with reality itself. They can't think straight anymore. Feeling no pain, they let themselves go in sexual obsession, addicted to every sort of perversion. But that's no life for you. You [have] learned Christ! My assumption is that you have paid careful attention to him and [have] been well instructed in the truth precisely as we have it in Jesus. Since, we do not have the excuse of ignorance, everything — and I do mean everything — that is connected with that old way of life has to go. It is rotten through and through. Get rid of it! And then take on an entirely new way of life — a God-fashioned life, a life renewed from the inside and working itself into your conduct as God accurately reproduces His Character in you."* (Ephesians 4:19-24 MSG)

> *". . . Reckon yourselves to be dead indeed to sin, but alive to God in Christ Jesus our Lord. And if Christ is in you, the body is dead because of sin, but the Spirit is life because of righteousness."*
> (Romans 6:11, 8:10 NKJV)

Disciples Indeed

> *". . . If ye continue in my word, then are ye my disciples indeed; and you shall know the truth and the truth shall make you free."*
>
> (John 8:31 KJV)

Remarkably, having just elaborated on "truth", we find that there is so much more. "Truth" brings freedom. I believe that a person who enjoys freedom epitomizes the character of Christ in the fullest measure. However, for the discussion at hand, we will focus on the word "continue". The Greek translation of the word "continue" is meno, and it means to remain and abide, not to depart, and to remain as one, not to become another or different. (See Strong's 3306). "Continue" also means that we are to persist, without giving up. There were seventy disciples whom Jesus had sent on a mission trip, and upon reporting back to Him about their accomplishments, they were excited because they had killed the giants, so to speak. Putting it in their words, they said, ". . . *even the devils are subject unto us through thy name!"* (Luke 10:17 KJV). We know that this was a brand-new experience for them, for had it not been, they would have had a spirit of expectation and would not have been taken by surprise. *"My soul, wait thou only upon God; for my expectation is from him,"* (Psalm 62:5 KJV). Nonetheless, we understand that they had to have been operating with some level of faith because they took a step and went out to evangelize the country. We also know that these disciples had been spending some sort of time with Christ Jesus and operated as believers because signs followed them through the Name of Jesus. It is my belief that some of them had not reached a level of faith sufficient enough to sustain themselves, for many died very cruel deaths. The Apostle James had his head cut off, and so was John the Baptist's head cut off while he was in prison (Matthew 14:1-3). I believe if these men had operated on a level of faith as

Paul and Silas did when they were in prison, God would have intervened and saved them, just as He did Paul and Silas. Instead of wailing, lamenting, howling, and bawling, Paul and Silas prayed and sang to God. They were caught up in the spirit and brought Heaven right down into that jail cell. Even the bricks, mortar, and steel bars could not contain them when the Holy Spirit came upon the scene. The Bible says:

> *"But at midnight Paul and Silas were praying and singing hymns to God, and the prisoners were listening to them. Suddenly there was a great earthquake, so that the foundations of the prison were shaken; and immediately all the doors were opened and everyone's chains were loosed. And the keeper of the prison, awaking from sleep and seeing the prison doors open, supposing the prisoners had fled, drew his sword and was about to kill himself. But Paul called with a loud voice, saying, 'Do yourself no harm, for we are all here.' Then he called for a light, ran in, and fell down trembling before Paul and Silas. And he brought them out and said, 'Sirs, what must I do to be saved?' "*
>
> (Acts 16:25-30 NKJV)

There are some martyrs whose lives, I believe, are destined for sacrifice. Stephen was stoned to death, but prior to his death, the heavens opened up to receive him. Stephen's most powerful message set forth a revolution and helped to transform lives for centuries to come. Bringing it closer to home, I align Stephen's death with the death of Dr. Martin Luther King. Many of us believe that Dr. King's life was destined for sacrifice. His mountaintop experience could be comparable to the heavens opening up for Steven because he proclaimed that he had been to the mountaintop but that he would not cross over, for longevity had its place. Stephen, as Jesus did, repented on behalf of his brothers, for they knew not what they were doing.

As a new Christian, it bothered me that some of the mightiest ministers of God died before they reached the age of 70. While in school, Dean Pickens told our class a story of a young, dynamic minister who ignored the nudging of the Holy Spirit and was consequently killed by an automobile because of his disobedience.

> *"The days of our years are threescore years and ten; and if by reason of strength they be fourscore years, yet is their strength labour and sorrow; for it is soon cut off, and we fly away."*
>
> (Psalms 90:10 KJV)

And:

> *"And the LORD said, My spirit shall not always strive with man, for that he also is flesh: yet his days shall be an hundred and twenty years."*
>
> (Genesis 6:3 KJV)

One commonly accepted view of Peter's death is that he was hanged upside down, symbolizing the death of Christ, but I cannot locate such scriptures in the Bible. We do know that Peter was fearful and impetuous — facts verified within scriptures. On one occasion, Peter proved impetuous when he cut off the ear of the soldier:

> *"Then Simon Peter, having a sword, drew it and struck the high priest's servant, and cut off his right ear. The servant's name was Malchus."*
>
> (John 18:10 NKJV)

On three recorded occasions, Peter displayed definite acts of "little faith". Jesus had warned Peter in advance that he would deny Him three times, and it is my belief that a forewarning is designed to help us to forearm. Generally, when we know what the future will bring, we gird up our loins, muster up a bit more confidence, and put on the whole armor of God. Yet, in Peter's case, he fell right into the devil's trap:

"Peter answered and said to Him, 'Even if all are made to stumble because of You, I will never be made to stumble.' Jesus said to him, 'Assuredly, I say to you that this night, before the rooster crows, you will deny Me three times.' Peter said to Him, 'Even if I have to die with You, I will not deny You!' And so said all the disciples."
(Matthew 26:33 NKJV)

". . . Then he began to curse and swear, saying, 'I do not know the Man!' Immediately a rooster crowed."
(Matthew 26:74 NKJV)

Peter denied Christ Jesus three times just as Jesus had prophesied. It seems to me that Jesus warning Peter would have taken root, since Peter was the only disciple who recognized Jesus as Christ, the Son of the Living God.

"When Jesus came into the region of Caesarea Philippi, He asked His disciples, saying, 'Who do men say that I, the Son of Man, am?' So they said, 'Some say John the Baptist, some Elijah, and others Jeremiah or one of the prophets.' He said to them, 'But who do you say that I am?' Simon Peter answered and said, 'You are the Christ, the Son of the living God.' "
(Matthew 16:13-16 NKJV)

And yet, even after that, Jesus, Himself, warned Peter that satan wanted to sift him as wheat.

"And the Lord said, 'Simon, Simon! Indeed, Satan has asked for you, that he may sift you as wheat.' "
(Luke 22:31 NKJV)

Another occasion where Peter failed to prove himself strong in faith was when Jesus had bade Peter to join Him and walk on the water.

> *"So He said, 'Come.' And when Peter had come down out of the boat, he walked on the water to go to Jesus. But when he saw that the wind was boisterous, he was afraid; and beginning to sink he cried out, saying, 'Lord, save me!' "*
>
> (Matthew 14:29-30 NKJV)

I contend that since Peter was a hotheaded individual, as displayed by the documented acts of spontaneity, he enjoyed proving to the crowd that he was a mighty man of valor. Many of us are like Peter. When we are with the church folks, we boast of the mighty power of God and how we trust Him. We go on group outings to witness in the community and to see the Hand of God at work. Some of us even see God's Hand working in and through us. (Remember, Judas was one of the initial 12 Disciples.) But when we are alone where there are no other Christians, it is as though the plug has been pulled, and the power of God has been disconnected — No current is flowing. The spirit of timidity shows up, and we become afraid to display that mighty power of God resting within us. In Peter's case, I find no evidence in the Bible where he died a sacrificial death in the sense of types and shadows where his death depicted the death of Jesus. In fact, Jesus told Peter that when he was old, he would be forced to go where he did not want to go.

> *"I assure you, most solemnly I tell you, when you were young you girded yourself [put on your own belt or girdle] and you walked about wherever you pleased to go. But when you grow old you will stretch out your hands, and someone else will put a girdle around you and carry you where you do not wish to go."*
>
> (John 21:18 AMP)

Countless commentaries have speculated as to what Jesus meant when He told Peter that when he grew old he would stretch forth his hands and somebody else would lead him where he did not wish to go.

> *"He said this to indicate by what kind of death Peter would glorify God."*
>
> (John 21:19 AMP)

In my opinion, any martyr's death is a death which glorifies God. After all, Peter had been a professional fisherman and had given up his career — and maybe his inheritance because it was a family business — to follow Christ. Peter led more souls to Christ than any other disciple after he was filled with the Holy Spirit. However, we see in Scripture where Jesus prophesied to Peter that his last days would be days of captivity. Where there is no freedom, there is bondage, and when there is bondage, the Holy Spirit does not have free rein to function. As such, I consider that Peter's final days were days of discontentment rather than joy in the Holy Ghost, as Paul and Silas displayed when they were led where they did not want to be led. I conclude that Peter had grown old and listless, and rather than giving up the ghost, he simply gave up.

Do you recall the story of Nora Lam? If ever you have an opportunity to watch the movie *China Cry*, by all means, do so. For a faith builder, it will be well worth your time to view this film. *China Cry* is a biographical film taken from Nora Lam's life story. It tells about the rise of the communist state in China. As the story progresses, Sung Neng Yee (Nora's name) is arrested by communist authorities and thrown in jail because of her Christianity. When she refuses to deny Jesus Christ, she is placed before a firing squadron. Bullets fly at Nora by the dozens, but not a single one is able to hit her. Why? Because she dwells in the secret place of the Most High and has angels protecting her. Not once does Nora deny God! Not once does she doubt His protection! God said only with our eyes will we behold the reward of the wicked one:

"He who dwells in the secret place of the Most High Shall abide under the shadow of the Almighty. I will say of the LORD, 'He is my refuge and my fortress; My God, in Him I will trust.' Surely He shall deliver you from the snare of the fowler And from the perilous pestilence. He shall cover you with His feathers, And under His wings you shall take refuge; His truth shall be your shield and buckler. You shall not be afraid of the terror by night, Nor of the arrow that flies by day, Nor of the pestilence that walks in darkness, Nor of the destruction that lays waste at noonday. A thousand may fall at your side, And ten thousand at your right hand; But it shall not come near you. Only with your eyes shall you look, And see the reward of the wicked. Because you have made the LORD, who is my refuge, Even the Most High, your dwelling place, No evil shall befall you, Nor shall any plague come near your dwelling; For He shall give His angels charge over you, To keep you in all your ways. In their hands they shall bear you up, Lest you dash your foot against a stone. You shall tread upon the lion and the cobra, The young lion and the serpent you shall trample underfoot. 'Because he has set his love upon Me, therefore I will deliver him; I will set him on high, because he has known My name. He shall call upon Me, and I will answer him; I will be with him in trouble; I will deliver him and honor him. With long life I will satisfy him, And show him My salvation.' "

(Psalm 91 NKJV)

Nora is taken to a labor camp while pregnant, but survives to take her children and family to freedom. Fear has torment, and when you stand strong in the face of death and destruction, God will always protect you. I'm sure fear must have made its attempt to overwhelm Nora when she was placed before the firing squad. Nora knew the power in the Name of Jesus, and as she spoke it, even if speaking softly as Hannah had when praying to God for her baby, fear had to leave.

I recall when a man in Chicago pointed a gun at me, swearing to kill me, but I pushed my finger through the heavy mist of fear and said, "In the Name of Jesus!" That's all I said before he sped off like a burning brush fire. If we are going to be Christians, then we are going to trust God's Word openly and completely, whether in a crowd or alone. Remember, God never leaves us. God will never allow sickness, danger, or evil to overtake a trusting child of His, and 99 times out of 100, it is a demon of fear that will trick us out of victory.

Also, some of the disciples' level of trust in Jesus was not sufficient to cause most of them to run the course, for we find that many of them turned their backs on Jesus.

> *"Know ye not that they which run in a race run all, but one receiveth the price? So run, that ye may obtain."*
> (1 Corinthians 9:24 KJV)

Being quick to begin a project doesn't bring you the reward; nor does it cause you to win or achieve. To "start" a course or project merely means to initiate or to begin. Just think in terms of when you began school. Where did you start? How much did you accomplish? Kindergarten or first grade will only launch a foundation, but what happens if you do not proceed? The matter of demons being subject to us is a foundational principle. *Notwithstanding in this rejoice not, that the spirits are subject unto you; but rather rejoice, because your names are written in heaven.* (Luke 10:20 NKV)

> *"Therefore leaving the principles of the doctrine of Christ, let us go on unto perfection; not laying again the foundation of repentance from dead works, and of faith toward God, Of the doctrine of baptisms, and of laying on of hands, and of resurrection of the dead, and of eternal judgment."*
> (Hebrews 6:1-2 KJV)

Jesus, Himself, said that the signs and wonders would follow the believer:

> *"And these signs shall follow them that believe; In my name shall they cast out devils; they shall speak with new tongues; They shall take up serpents; and if they drink any deadly thing, it shall not hurt them; they shall lay hands on the sick, and they shall recover."*
> (Mark 16:17-18 KJV)

Faith is merely acting on God's Word, and taking a step of faith will produce evidence that the Word is alive.

> *"For the word of God is alive and powerful. It is sharper than the sharpest two-edged sword, cutting between soul and spirit, between joint and marrow. It exposes our innermost thoughts and desires."*
> (Hebrews 4:12 AMP)

God wants us to go on to maturity (Hebrews 6:1-2). He wants us to follow the example that Jesus left, so that we will not simply be identified as believers, but as disciples.

On at least two occasions I've heard believers argue that there is a difference in the terms "perfect" and "mature", when, in essence, these words are synonymous. From the King James Version of the Bible, Strong's Concordance translates "perfect" as being *complete and entire* (See 2522). While the word "mature" does not appear in the King James Version, it does in the New King James Version, and in countless instances has been translated with the word "perfect". Under www.definitions.net, mature is defined as the following: *"Is brought by natural process to completeness of growth and development; fitted by growth and development for any function, action, or state, appropriate to its kind; full-grown; ripe."*

"Disciples indeed" escalate beyond the position of mere believers. Remember, many are called, but few are chosen

(Matthew 22:14). Remember, also, that believing is not enough, because devils believe and tremble. *"Thou believest that there is one God, thou doest well: the devils also believe, and tremble,"* (James 2:19 KJV). The fact that the Apostle James classifies devils in a category with believers ought to make us shudder. It's no wonder there have been given two definitions of completely opposite meanings for the word 'fear': reverential fear toward and for God, and trembling, tormented fear from the devil. Notice, our reverential worshipping fear goes *to* God, but the fear that torments comes *from* the devil. This alone should cause us to stop and ask, "Who's in charge?" Are we giving or receiving? Look at this in a new perspective and let's ask ourselves, "Are we demonstrating the power Jesus has given to us, or are we behaving as Adam behaved by giving our power away?" Most of us say that we believe the Word of God, yet, God is waiting for us to become what we believe. Will we allow ourselves to be deceived also? Are we being tricked?

A Lukewarm Mind is a Sick Mind

"Let not him that is deceived trust in vanity: for vanity shall be his recompence."

(Job 15:31 KJV)

"Know ye not that the unrighteous shall not inherit the kingdom of God? Be not deceived: neither fornicators, nor idolaters, nor adulterers, nor effeminate, nor abusers of themselves with mankind."

(1 Corinthians 6:9 KJV)

At the time Jesus sent the Twelve Disciples on the mission field, Judas was among them. Judas saw the lame become able to walk, the blind have their eyes opened, and even the dead come back to life. But the problem with Judas was that he had one foot in and the other out. Judas was a lukewarm Christian, and those who are lukewarm are an abomination to God, because He promises to spue (spit out) the lukewarm out of His mouth (Revelation 3:16). Lukewarm Christians are the same as Christians who stagger, and Jesus calls them lukewarm because they are comfortable living in their spurious state of illusion. Those who live in an unauthentic state bear the same symptoms of those who are mentally ill:

> *To be mentally ill by definition, however, is to be given a diagnosis of a common debilitating mental weakness by a professional mental health worker. In the United States, a full 40% of the population has received a diagnosis of mental illness sometime in their lives.*
>
> *Being mentally ill means:*
>
> *Thinking outside of "normal" rational concepts, causing you not to participate in a normal life.*
>
> *For a portion of one's life, it is the inability to make one's own choices based on what makes the most sense to them.*
>
> *Possibly thinking self-destructive thoughts or do[ing] things that are self-destructive.*
>
> *Sometimes having an inability to understand what people are saying to you and are [being] not able to control your own behavior.*
>
> *Having others be exasperated with you or treat you like a child.*
>
> *Often not understanding the motivation for one's own deeds or speech.*
>
> *Constantly regretting one's actions, but not knowing what to do about it. (www.nowheretolayhishead.org)*

When a person lives in a state of illusion, he or she is no different than the person who is mentally ill, because both operate within the boundaries of unfounded actions. Here we have Judas, a man chosen by Jesus to help populate the world with the promised gift of eternal life and divine prosperity (which includes health, safety, protection, provision, etc,), and he chooses to forsake all by betraying Jesus. Jesus had shared mysteries with Judas . . . mysteries that no other leader could know, perform, or promise, yet he chose to turn his back on the most phenomenal person who ever walked the face of the Earth. Judas was lukewarm. Lukewarm people don't know who they are, so they flow in any direction to please anybody, never remaining loyal to anyone, not even to themselves. Lukewarm Christians will assume the character, beliefs, and opinions of the person they are appeasing *at the time*, too afraid and insecure to stand for truth. These people are in bondage with no insight of truth.

Jesus calls these unstable Christians lukewarm. When I think of "lukewarm", I associate it with water. How many times have I immersed myself in lukewarm water and felt perfectly satisfied? Lukewarm water is so-o-o soothing that when we immerse ourselves in it, we want to just sit there and not move, feeling that everything is perfectly fine. It's the same with lukewarm Christians. Most of them, in fact, think that they're all right: they think everything's good, and there is nothing else that needs to be done in their lives. This is a scary position to find oneself in, especially when the curtain is drawn.

Let's take a look at the water: If the water is too hot, it will scald you, leaving you burned and blistered. If it's too cold, it will freeze and turn to ice, causing frostbite or worse.

Too hot, you're set ablaze, burning with fire from the Holy Ghost. All of the impurities are burned out, and no more dross settles at the root of any part of your being. You become purged, refined, and pure. You become so desirable that the whole world gravitates toward you. And not only the whole world, but God, Himself, because you have chosen not to compromise your relationship with Him, so He sits as a refiner and purifier and purges you more and more, making you prepared to be His Son's bride.

> *"And he shall sit as a refiner and purifier of silver: and he shall purify the sons of Levi, and purge them as gold and silver, that they may offer unto the LORD an offering in righteousness."*
>
> (Malachi 3:3 KJV)

Too cold, you freeze and become as hard as a rock. Your heart is hardened; your body is stiff. Not even a bubble can float inside of you to make foamy suds to wash your heart. There is no room for love or compassion for others. Most of these folks call themselves either agnostics or atheists. This is where the love of many wax cold (Matthew 24:12). A hardened heart, God wants no parts of, because a hardened heart wants no parts of God, for *". . . if we deny him, he also will deny us,"* (2 Timothy 2:12 KJV). And though claiming to be an agnostic or atheist (There is no genuine atheist because John 1:9 (KJV) says, *"That was the true Light, which lighteth every man that cometh into the world."*), at least everyone knows where the person who is cold stands. There is neither doubt nor ambiguity about the relationship this person has with Christ, which means that this person is no hypocrite. Hot or cold, you are either of your Father, God, or your father, the devil.

> *"Ye are of your father the devil, and the lusts of your father ye will do. He was a murderer from the beginning, and abode not in the truth, because there is no truth in him. When he speaketh a lie, he speaketh of his own: for he is a liar, and the father of it."*
>
> (John 8:44 KJV)

But the lukewarm saint is a far more serious matter. This is a bad apple that will cause the entire bushel of apples to rot. Demon-satan will see to it that the newly-converted Christians migrate to the lukewarm saint, so that their understanding of true Christianity is perverted. Lukewarm Christians destroy the lives of other Christians. Not only do they destroy the lives of immature Christians, but they also discourage other prospects from joining the Christian family. After all, why should they become Christians when the Christians they know live disrespectful, untrustworthy, unfruitful, and unholy lives? Lukewarm Christians are and will continue to be easily deceived:

> *"But evil men and seducers shall wax worse and worse,*
> *deceiving, and being deceived . . ."*
> (2 Timothy 3:13 KJV)

If you recall, Judas was a regular churchgoer who operated in the gifts of the Spirit, and he was a part of the in-crowd when it was time for wining and dining. Yet, with all of his inner connections, he was deceived and met with everlasting destruction. Judas was lukewarm.

WHEN A PERSON LIVES IN A STATE OF ILLUSION HE OR SHE IS NO DIFFERENT THAN THE PERSON WHO IS MENTALLY ILL BECAUSE BOTH OPERATE WITHIN THE BOUNDARIES OF UNFOUNDED ACTIONS.

A lukewarm mind is a sick mind, which parallels with the mind of an insane individual, and it self-destructs. Lukewarm Christians are tricked into sickness. In the case of Judas, this sickness caused him to kill himself, and that is satan's ultimate goal: our self-destruction.

"For if we sin willfully after we have received the knowledge of the truth, there no longer remains a sacrifice for sins, but a certain fearful expectation of judgment, and fiery indignation which will devour the adversaries. Anyone who has rejected Moses' law dies without mercy on the testimony of two or three witnesses. Of how much worse punishment, do you suppose, will he be thought worthy who has trampled the Son of God underfoot, counted the blood of the covenant by which he was sanctified a common thing, and insulted the Spirit of grace? For we know Him who said, 'Vengeance is Mine, I will repay,' says the Lord. And again, 'The LORD will judge His people.' It is a fearful thing to fall into the hands of the living God."

(Hebrews 10:26-31 NKJV)

I believe that this is the hour when we must reverently and wholeheartedly love, honor, cherish, protect, and promote the precious and sacred Gospel of Christ Jesus our Lord and Savior. Prior to the many disciples turning away, Jesus had explained to them the price they would have to pay in order to become true disciples:

"This is the bread which cometh down from heaven, that a man may eat thereof, and not die. I am the living bread which came down from heaven: if any man eat of this bread, he shall live for ever: and the bread that I will give is my flesh, which I will give for the life of the world. The Jews therefore strove among themselves, saying, How can this man give us his flesh to eat? Then Jesus said unto them, Verily, verily, I say unto you, Except ye eat the flesh of the Son of man, and drink his blood, ye have no life in you. Whoso eateth my flesh, and drinketh my blood, hath eternal life; and I will raise him up at the last day. For my flesh is meat indeed, and my blood is drink indeed. He

*that eateth my flesh, and drinketh my blood, dwelleth in
me, and I in him. As the living Father hath sent me, and I
live by the Father: so he that eateth me, even he shall live
by me. This is that bread which came down from heaven:
not as your fathers did eat manna, and are dead: he that
eateth of this bread shall live for ever. These things said
he in the synagogue, as he taught in Capernaum. Many
therefore of his disciples, when they had heard this, said,
This is a hard saying; who can hear it."*

(John 6:50-60 KJV)

The bread Jesus referred to was His flesh, meaning His life, which He was surrendering for the sin of the world. The price Jesus paid was not simply an atonement or a covering up for our sins, as the animal skin used for Adam and Eve's covering when they were in the Garden, *"For it is not possible that the blood of bulls and of goats should take away sins,"* (Hebrews 10:4 KJV). But through His sacrificial death on the Cross, Christ Jesus became a substitute or propitiation for the sin of all humankind. *"And He Himself is the propitiation for our sins, and not for ours only but also for the whole world,"* (1 John 2:2 NKJV). To substitute means to take the place of. When the new takes the place of the old, the old is wiped out and becomes nonexistent. When we eat the flesh of Jesus, He then lives in us, *"For in him we live, and move, and have our being; as certain also of your own poets have said, For we are also his offspring,"* (Acts 17:28 KJV). Now, we are being nourished with the bread of eternal life because Jesus is the bread of life. When we drink of His Blood, we are being reminded that His precious Blood has washed away all of our sins, and not only our sins, but the sin of the world. In other words, the entire penalty for sin was placed on Jesus' body when He went to the Cross and died for all sinners. Through His death, we can all be free from sin because the price has been paid.

All Jesus asked was that the disciples partake in the grace resulting from the sacrifice He was about to make on their

45

behalf. Because these followers had voluntarily chosen to follow Christ, Jesus thought it not robbery to repay them by assuring them that eternal life was theirs, and they would never hunger or thirst. He was offering them the bread of life, and complete redemption through His Blood. However, many thought the rich and immeasurable offer was too much for them to accept. That's because they were operating in head knowledge. No doubt, many of them had promised Jesus that they would follow him, but they had not stopped to count the cost. They had taken into consideration only what would benefit them at the time, and they had no spiritual discernment. They said, *"This is a hard thing, who can hear it?"* The god of this world, satan, had hidden the good news from them: *"But if our gospel be hid, it is hid to them that are lost: In whom the god of this world hath blinded the minds of them which believe not, lest the light of the glorious gospel of Christ, who is the image of God, should shine unto them,"* (2 Corinthians 4:3-4 KJV). Then said Jesus unto the twelve, "Will ye also go away?" (John 6:67)

Unlike those who had walked away from Jesus, Peter had not only seen Jesus' acts, but he had also learned His ways. Peter knew that Jesus was the Savior of the world. "Then Simon Peter answered him, Lord, to whom shall we go? Thou hast the words of eternal life."

And we believe and are sure that thou art that Christ, the Son of the living God." (John 6:68-9) Flesh and blood did not reveal this to Peter; he could only have known this through revelation knowledge from God.

Not much has changed today. Those who have a personal relationship with God understand that there is no other place to go except to Him, and His main headquarters are His Word and prayer. I apologize for not being able to credit the author, but I either read or heard this question: "How much of God do you want?" And the answer, "You want as much as you have." God will never withhold Himself from us; in fact, He is so hungry for our love and affection that He has labeled us His bride, long before the wedding supper. That's faith unfeigned.

The seventy disciples began in Jesus' presence. They saw the works of God through the Name of Jesus, yet, past their initial experience, we don't hear anymore about them. They were like severed branches from a tree, no sap from which to drink, and all withered away. One who continues in God's Word develops such a hunger for God that there is no tasteful desire for worldly concerns. Such a person "*. . . have no fellowship with the unfruitful works of darkness, but rather reprove them,*" (Ephesians 5:11 KJV) and places God first in all things.

Mind you, unless you make yourself available to satan, he has no place in you. After all, your adversary the devil walks about as a roaring lion seeking whom he may devour. If the devil has to look for someone to devour, it means that there are many he must bypass because they are not ignorant of satan's devices, and they have closed the door to his tactics.

God has designed and equipped us to rule over everything from diseases to disasters and every other bad thing in-between. But to do so, we must mature and become disciples, indeed. Stagnated Christians create barriers to spiritual growth and remain infants in Christ, and God is tutoring us. The Message translation puts it this way, giving a bit more impetus to the stagnated Christian:

> *"No prolonged infancies among us, please. We'll not tolerate babes in the woods or small children who are an easy prey for impostors. God wants us to grow up, to know the whole truth and tell it in love—like Christ in everything. We take our lead from Christ, who is the source of everything we do. He keeps us in step with each other. His very breath and blood flows through us, nourishing us so that we will grow up healthy in God, robust in love."*
>
> (Ephesians 4:14-16 MSG)

I cannot overly emphasize that the Bible is not simply a good book. It is imperative that you know, without a fleeting doubt, that the Bible is the inerrant voice of the living God. Anyone can write a good book, such as the one you are now reading, but the Bible is God's voice, speaking to His people through His prophets.

> *"All scripture is given by inspiration of God [God-breathed], and is profitable for doctrine, for reproof, for correction, for instruction in righteousness: That the man of God may be perfect thoroughly furnished unto all good works."*
>
> (2 Timothy 3:16-17 KJV, note added)

The heart of God longs for His children to lift His Words from the recorded pages of the Book and cause them to live and move and have their very being projected from the inside of them to change the outside world. Why do you suppose Jesus promises that signs and wonders will follow the Word?

> *"And these signs shall follow them that believe, In my name shall they cast out devils, and they shall speak with new tongues, They shall take up serpents, and if they drink any deadly thing, it shall not hurt them; they shall lay hands on the sick, and they shall recover. So then after the Lord had spoken unto them, he was received up into heaven, and sat on the right hand of God. And they went forth, and preached every where, the Lord working with them, and confirming the word with signs following. Amen."*
>
> (Mark 16:17-20 KJV)

When God's Word is spoken in belief, the spoken Word becomes life, and God, Himself, is presented again (represented) through His disciples. In this hour, more than ever before, God is seeking animated, brio believers who will cause His Words to flash from spirit to life.

". . . the words that I speak unto you, they are spirit, and they are life."
(John 6:63 KJV)

"For the eyes of the LORD run to and fro throughout the whole earth, to show Himself strong on behalf of those whose heart is loyal to Him . . ."
(2 Chronicles 16:9 NKJV)

"For with God nothing shall be impossible."
(Luke 1:37 KJV)

". . . for with God all things are possible."
(Mark 10:27 KJV)

". . . and nothing shall be impossible unto you."
(Matthew 17:20 KJV)

There are other similar promises, motivating us to go on to the fullness of the measure of the stature of Christ Jesus. In summary, God has enabled man to take the Words from His mouth and put them on pages, and from these pages (the Bible) into his mouth, so that they will be permeated throughout the Earth and be perpetuated throughout all generations. The Word of God is God (1 John 5:7), and leaving us His Word is one of the most attainable measures God has chosen for His people to get to know Him intimately, and to produce after His own kind.

The Apostle Paul was one of the most prolific and learned men of his day, having been taught at the feet of Gamaliel, according to the perfect manner of the law. Yet, after He was converted on the Damascus Road, Paul conceded, *"Yea doubtless, and I count all things but loss for the excellency of the knowledge of Christ Jesus my Lord: for whom I have suffered the loss of all things, and do count them but dung, that I may win Christ . . . That I may know him, and the power of his resurrection and the fellowship of his sufferings being made conformable unto his death."* (Philippians 3:8,10 KJV)

There were Twelve Disciples before Paul, yet Paul was the trailblazer who did not just *write* two-thirds of the New Testament. The Apostle Paul set a pattern for us to follow in alignment with his writings, as well as the Old Testament psalmist. Paul said, *"For I am now ready to be offered, and the time of my departure is at hand. I have fought a good fight, I have finished my course, I have kept the faith,"* (2 Timothy 4:6-7 KJV). All of the attempts on Paul's life meant absolutely nothing to him because his heart-cry was to know God with all excellence, nothing wavering. No sickness could cause Paul to succumb to death, because Paul knew that at the Name of Jesus sickness had to bow its foul knee. As it is written, *"That at the name of Jesus every knee should bow, of things in heaven, and things in earth, and things under the earth,"* (Philippians 2:10 KJV). Paul understood with his heart and not his head, that death had no control over him because God told us that death had lost its sting.

> *"O death, where is thy sting? O grave, where is thy victory? The sting of death is sin; and the strength of sin is the law. But thanks be to God, which giveth us the victory through our Lord Jesus Christ."*
> (1 Corinthians 15:55-57 KJV)

No man could take Paul's life, because he had sought Christ and had learned how to number his own days, a lesson he learned from the psalmist:

> *"So teach us to number our days, that we may apply our hearts unto wisdom."*
> (Psalm 90:12 KJV)

Paul was a man of great understanding, and he also knew how to move in God's times and seasons. At the proper time, Paul knew that he would be ready to offer up his life, and not a second before.

"Daniel answered and said, Blessed be the name of God for ever and ever: for wisdom and might are his: And he changeth the times and the seasons: he removeth kings, and setteth up kings: he giveth wisdom unto the wise, and knowledge to them that know understanding: He revealeth the deep and secret things: he knoweth what is in the darkness, and the light dwelleth with him."

(Daniel 2:20-22 KJV)

"But without faith it is impossible to please him (God)... and he (God) is a rewarder of them that diligently seek him."

(Hebrews 11:6 KJV)

After Paul's conversion, his entire life was a life of faith, and he understood what it meant to please God by walking his life out in faith. Paul also understood the joy that awaited him once his earthly course was finished. After all, he had enjoyed many heavenly visitations. In Acts 26:19, while presenting his case to King Agrippa, Paul informed the king that he was not disobedient to "the heavenly vision", referring to his Damascus Road experience where God blinded his eyes and gave him a heavenly vision, transforming his life. Another example of Paul's heavenly vision:

"This boasting will do no good, but I must go on. I will reluctantly tell about visions and revelations from the Lord. I was caught up to the third heaven fourteen years ago. Whether I was in my body or out of my body, I don't know—only God knows. Yes, only God knows whether I was in my body or outside my body. But I do know that I was caught up to paradise and heard things so astounding that they cannot be expressed in words, things no human is allowed to tell."

(2 Corinthians 12:1-5 NLT)

Heavenly visions in the Bible are given to us for examples, to let us know that we, too, can have a relationship with God so closely that He will permit us to visit His home. Isn't that what close friends and family do, visit each other?

Paul believed what was written, and the Spirit of the Word living in his spirit caused the Word to come alive. The key is, you must believe that God *is* His Word. You must understand that all God has written to us is for our benefit, to prepare us to experience and enjoy our inheritance, as His dear children. You must know that God's Kingdom resides and rests inside your body.

> *"Neither shall they say, Lo here! or, lo there! for, behold,*
> *the kingdom of God is within you."*
>
> (Luke 17:21 KJV)

One of the youngest persons I have heard of who went to Heaven is internationally renown historian and author, Pastor Roberts Liardon. Roberts' mother raised her son in a manner that I implore all young mothers to follow: she assigned him scripture reading of four chapters daily from the Bible, when he was barely old enough to read. It paid off, big. Roberts Liardon has been ministering since he was twelve years old. At the precious age of eight years old, God honored this child with a heavenly experience. As Pastor Liardon conveys the story, he says that Jesus literally dunked him under the water in the River of Life, and that's when the fun began, with Jesus and Roberts splashing water from one to the other, enjoying a great water fight. Roberts explains that when he was in the water, it was like no other water he had ever experienced. Rather than water surrounding him, it was as if the water's energy was flowing throughout his entire being. It makes sense to me: the Bible says that out of our bellies shall flow rivers of living water:

> *"He that believeth on me, as the scripture hath said, out*
> *of his belly shall flow rivers of living water."*
>
> (John 7:38 KJV)

It seems as though Roberts was swimming in the "River of Life" and it was "life" from that river penetrating his entire body — simply attesting to the significance of the title of the River of Life. I don't find it surprising at all that in Heaven the River of Life surges through one's body when swimming. I believe it is an indication that everlasting life is within you. Earth is only a shadow of Heaven, giving us a glimpse of what is to come. Everything in Heaven exists beyond our earthly comprehension.

Not only was Heaven a fun time for Roberts, but God showed Roberts a building that contained all types of human body parts. When showing him the body parts, Jesus told him that the parts were "unclaimed blessings". God explained to him that the body parts did not belong in Heaven, and Heaven's doors were always open, just waiting for us to claim these body parts or blessings. He saw hundreds of new eyes, ears, skin, even hair, and all it takes for us to get these body parts is faith — simple, childlike faith. When I read Roberts' heavenly experience, I thought of the Book of Ephesians:

> *"May blessing (praise, laudation, and eulogy) be to the God and Father of our Lord Jesus Christ (the Messiah) Who has blessed us in Christ with every spiritual (given by the Holy Spirit) blessing in the heavenly realm!"*
> (Ephesians 1:3 AMP)

It is clear from the Word of God that God wants to make all of His children whole. God loves us so much that He will take a little child like Roberts Liardon and give him a tour of Heaven just to bring Heaven's message back to Earth to attest to the authenticity of His Word.

The more of Him (the Bible) you pour into yourself, the more power you store up. However, just as the light bulb doesn't produce light until the switch is turned on, God's power stored inside of you cannot be revealed and experienced until you open your mouth and let it out. Your mouth represents the switch, and keeping it closed only builds the power inside of you if you have been diligent in reading the Word. Opening your mouth and speaking God's Word causes that power within you to be released. Command every mountain to be removed from your life as well as your body and you will witness God's Word as "life". Now, you will cause all adversities to be invaded by the supernatural and every ungodly situation is destroyed. Now, you will understand that you do not have to be tricked into sickness, and divine health belongs to you. God's Kingdom is in you, but only when what is in you is released will you become that light of the world.

So, first things first: knowing the matchless power of the authenticity of God's Word, and knowing that limitless power is in you, once you have equipped yourself with God's Word. The Word residing dormant is not enough. You must verbally and with authority begin to confess the Word so that you are able to experience all that Jesus did and more. A good instructor teaches. A great instructor not only teaches, but he or she leaves you experiencing what has been taught. A masterful instructor teaches, causes you to experience what has been taught, and also causes you to replicate himself or herself in the person of you, with the ability to build exponentially upon what has been lived. Jesus was a master teacher. And, as evidenced by the definition of masterful, Paul, having been taught of Gamaliel and also having been taught of Jesus, was a master teacher, and without discrediting Gamaiel, the scholar of Paul's day, all that Gamaliel taught Paul was placed on the back burner once Paul became a walking epistle read of men.

"Ye are our epistle written in our hearts, known and read of all men."

(2 Corinthians 3:2 KJV)

54

God's Word is alive, and once it has been saturated throughout your body, its irresistible power is known by all, whether intentional or not. That's what Paul means when he writes that you are walking epistles. Wherever you are and wherever you go, the love of God stamped in your heart brings forth an iridescent glow about your countenance causing your light to shine. You stand out in any crowd.

> *"Ye are the light of the world. A city that is set on an hill cannot be hid."*
> (Matthew 5:14 KJV)

Many will search you out for healing and deliverance, and you will shine as the brightness of the firmament, not just when God grants you your rewards, but right here on Earth because you have learned the secret of the mysteries of God's Word.

> *"And they that be wise shall shine as the brightness of the firmament; and they that turn many to righteousness as the stars for ever and ever."*
> (Daniel 12:3 KJV)

Those who are working for satan will relent, repent, and get saved, or they will take flight and vacate your territory, for the intensity of God's light always extinguishes darkness. Either way, all men will know who you are. It doesn't necessarily mean that all will fully understand your calling, but they will know that you are different.

> *"But ye are a chosen generation, a royal priesthood, a holy nation, a peculiar people; that ye should shew forth the praises of him who has called you out of darkness into His marvelous light."*
> (1 Peter 2:9 KJV)

One of the seven Spirits of God is named the Spirit of Might. As you read the Word of God, His Word is being imbedded into your mind and your spirit. You are pouring the Spirit of Might into your very own spirit . . . the real you, making you more and more like God and empowering your spirit to develop more and more into the likeness of His Spirit. The more you pour the Word of God into yourself, the more of His power you receive, and now the Spirit of Holiness becomes more and more profound in and about you. Now you are in a place where only Godliness resides, because His Spirit has been infused into your spirit. No more fears, no more doubts, and no more compromise — only God. And, because God is love, you are now totally embodied with love, and it becomes a robust love. All of God's Word is pure and real, and now, it's all interlocked within you, ready to move forward and demonstrate to the world just who God is. It is no longer you, but Christ in you. The Word has become flesh, just as it became flesh when God met Mary and impregnated her with Jesus. The Word in you impregnates you, and when brought forth, it enables you to do exactly what Jesus did, and more. Your heart is engulfed with love, and all worldly attributes and raiders vanish, when overpowered with the Spirit of Christ. If, per chance, invaders called 'infirmities' were trespassing in your body, they must leave because no sickness can remain where the Spirit of Might with His robust love dwells and rules.

> *"Verily, verily, I say unto you, He that believeth on me, the works that I do shall he do also; and greater works than these shall he do; because I go unto my Father."*
> (John 14:12 KJV)

I have a bit of unrest with folks who water down God's Word. There are many who will attempt to bring God down to their level, to accommodate their deficiencies, physically, mentally, and otherwise. Many times I've heard folks say that the greater works in John 12:14 means that we would do more in numbers, which means that since Jesus only spent 3½ years ministering here on Earth, He could only perform so many miracles. While this conclusion has a bit of truth, it certainly does not seize all of what Jesus documented. I think if this was the case, Jesus would probably have said that we would do "more" works than He had done. Why do so many of we Christians entertain the limitations introduced to our finite minds? God forbid!

Certainly we will do more in numbers, because just as the world today is more heavily populated than it was back in 30 AD, so are God's disciples greater in numbers. We must remember that when Christ Jesus performed His earthly ministry, God sent Him here in the person of a man to leave an example of what God expects from us. It is evident that most of us have been given far more than 3½ years to spread the Gospel of Christ, but this, also, is only a part of the truth. According to Strong's Concordance 3187 meizon (pronounced ma-zon), the definition of the word "greater" is greater, larger, elder, stronger. The Greek word "meizon" is taken from Strong's 3173, whose root word is "megas", and the outline of Bible usage as written in Blue Letter Bible states as follows — I'm listing the entire outline because I endeavor to emphasize Jesus' heart when He informs His disciples of their aspiration:

1) great
   a) of the external form or sensible appearance of things (or of persons)

2) in particular, of space and its dimensions, as respects
   a) mass and weight: great
   b) compass and extent: large, spacious
   c) measure and height: long
   d) stature and age: great, old
   e) of number and quantity: numerous, large, abundant
   f) of age: the elder
   g) used of intensity and its degrees: with great effort, of the affections and emotions of the mind, of natural events powerfully affecting the senses: violent, mighty, strong

3) predicated of rank, as belonging to
   a) persons, eminent for ability, virtue, authority, power
   b) things esteemed highly for their importance: of great moment, of great weight, importance
   c) a thing to be highly esteemed for its excellence: excellent

4) splendid, prepared on a grand scale, stately
   a) great things
   b) of God's preeminent blessings
   c) of things which overstep the province of a created being, proud (presumptuous) things, full of arrogance, derogatory to the majesty of God

Taking into consideration all of the explanations or definitions above for the word "greater" as Jesus uses it in John 14:12, it appears highly unlikely that Jesus was differentiating between the quality of works and the quantity of works that His disciples would perform. The descriptions of the word begin with dimensions as it relates to weights, measures, heights, and sizes in measurements as in borders and circumferences. The definition includes stature and age, for as we pointed out, Jesus' Earth ministry only lasted 3½ years prior to His ascension to the Father. The same meanings include number, quantity, large, abundant, and then proceed to intensity to its degrees with great effort of the affections and emotions of the mind; natural events powerfully affecting the senses; violent, mighty, strong persons, eminent for ability, virtue, authority, power, etc., as you can see. In light of these authoritative descriptions of the word "greater", as Jesus uses it here in John 14:12, we find that Jesus did not exclude any characteristic of the word "greater" within either realm of speculation, whether it be quantity or quality.

As the heavens are higher than the Earth, so are God's Ways higher than ours, and His thoughts higher than our thoughts, as He declares in Isaiah 55:9. God knows when we need to receive clarity, and when we do, He breaks the Word down for us, as He did with His disciples on many occasions when He taught them by using parables. (A good example is found in Mark, Chapter 4, when explaining the parable of the seed.) I marvel at Jesus' exactness. Greater is greater no matter how you look at it.

Therefore, first and foremost, trust God's Word and receive it word for word as it is written. The Bible interprets itself and has never been found to be in error. Do not accept a watered down version of God's Word and do not argue with those who do. Christ Jesus healed the sick, raised the dead, opened blind eyes, caused the lame to walk, the deaf to hear, fed the hungry, and according to the Gospel of John, *"And there are also many other things which Jesus did, the which, if they should be written every one, I suppose that even the world itself could not contain the books that should be written."* (John 21:25)

On two occasions, it is recorded that Jesus came back to Earth to speak with His disciples. When Christ Jesus rose from the grave, He appeared unto Mary Magdalene and the other Mary, telling them to run and tell the disciples that He would meet them in Galilee. Here is an account of Jesus' appearance:

> *"And, behold, there was a great earthquake: for the angel of the Lord descended from heaven, and came and rolled back the stone from the door, and sat upon it. His countenance was like lightning, and his raiment white as snow: And for fear of him the keepers did shake, and became as dead men. And the angel answered and said unto the women, Fear not ye: for I know that ye seek Jesus, which was crucified. He is not here: for he is risen, as he said. Come, see the place where the Lord lay. And go quickly, and tell his disciples that he is risen from the dead; and, behold, he goeth before you into Galilee; there shall ye see him: lo, I have told you. And they departed quickly from the sepulchre with fear and great joy; and did run to bring his disciples word. And as they went to tell his disciples, behold, Jesus met them, saying, All hail.*

And they came and held him by the feet, and worshipped him. Then said Jesus unto them, Be not afraid: go tell my brethren that they go into Galilee, and there shall they see me. Now when they were going, behold, some of the watch came into the city, and shewed unto the chief priests all the things that were done. And when they were assembled with the elders, and had taken counsel, they gave large money unto the soldiers, Saying, Say ye, His disciples came by night, and stole him away while we slept. And if this come to the governor's ears, we will persuade him, and secure you. So they took the money, and did as they were taught: and this saying is commonly reported among the Jews until this day. Then the eleven disciples went away into Galilee, into a mountain where Jesus had appointed them. And when they saw him, they worshipped him: but some doubted. And Jesus came and spake unto them, saying, All power is given unto me in heaven and in earth. Go ye therefore, and teach all nations, baptizing them in the name of the Father, and of the Son, and of the Holy Ghost."

(Matthew 28:2-19 KJV)

Again, Jesus appeared to His disciples in Jerusalem:

"And, behold, two of them went that same day to a village called Emmaus, which was from Jerusalem about threescore furlongs. And they talked together of all these things which had happened. And it came to pass, that, while they communed together and reasoned, Jesus himself drew near, and went with them. But their eyes were holden that they should not know him. And he said unto them, What manner of communications are these that ye have one to another, as ye walk, and are sad? And the one of them, whose name was Cleopas, answering said unto him, Art thou only a stranger in Jerusalem, and hast not known the things which are come to pass there

in these days? And he said unto them, What things? And they said unto him, Concerning Jesus of Nazareth, which was a prophet mighty in deed and word before God and all the people: And how the chief priests and our rulers delivered him to be condemned to death, and have crucified him. But we trusted that it had been he which should have redeemed Israel: and beside all this, to day is the third day since these things were done. Yea, and certain women also of our company made us astonished, which were early at the sepulchre; And when they found not his body, they came, saying, that they had also seen a vision of angels, which said that he was alive. And certain of them which were with us went to the sepulchre, and found it even so as the women had said: but him they saw not. Then he said unto them, O fools, and slow of heart to believe all that the prophets have spoken: Ought not Christ to have suffered these things, and to enter into his glory? And beginning at Moses and all the prophets, he expounded unto them in all the scriptures the things concerning himself. And they drew nigh unto the village, whither they went: and he made as though he would have gone further. But they constrained him, saying, Abide with us: for it is toward evening, and the day is far spent. And he went in to tarry with them. And it came to pass, as he sat at meat with them, he took bread, and blessed it, and brake, and gave to them. And their eyes were opened, and they knew him; and he vanished out of their sight. And they said one to another, Did not our heart burn within us, while he talked with us by the way, and while he opened to us the scriptures? And they rose up the same hour, and returned to Jerusalem, and found the eleven gathered together, and them that were with them, Saying, The Lord is risen indeed, and hath appeared to Simon. And they told what things were done in the way, and how he was known of them in breaking of bread."

(Luke 24:13-35 KJV)

John wrote that the "world" could not contain the books of all that Jesus did were it written (John 21:25). Consider today, saints of God, such a person as Katie Souza, whom the Holy Spirit has taught how to destroy wicked kings, and how to ascend into Heaven to get revelation and bring it back to Earth. Katie discovered what she calls the king-killer anointing: get the head, cut it off, and all the little-bitty demons underneath the head have to flee in fear. As you continue reading, you will find that where the head leads, the body follows — that's any head and any body, physical or spiritual. There is a king-demon of sickness and diseases as well as of fear and other ailments or maladies. Demons have rank, as described in Ephesians 6. You must get rid of top demons who have strong holds over your life, and all the other demons will flee. Jesus said to take out the strongman, and you can destroy his house.

Similar to Enoch having developed his faith to a point of deciding that He wanted to leave Earth and join God forever, for it was "... *by faith Enoch was translated that he should not see death; and was not found, because God had translated him; for before his translation, he had this testimony, that he pleased God,*" (Hebrews 11:5 KJV). God is welcoming His saints to ascend and descend to and from Heaven at will, to bring heavenly messages and equipment to Earth. God is no respecter of persons, and since He is the same yesterday and today and forever, He is also welcoming us to ascend to Heaven and remain, just as Enoch did.

The out-of-body experience I had cannot compare with Enoch's, because I am back here on Earth. But it was a most electrifying experience to have Jesus carry me in His arms and dance with me on the seashore. The simplicity of ascending to Heaven comes with a meager price of fasting, praying, and studying God's Word.

"Pray without ceasing."

(KJV)

"And he spake a parable unto them to this end, that men ought always to pray, and not to faint."

(Luke 18:1 KJV)

"Behold, ye fast for strife and debate, and to smite with the fist of wickedness: ye shall not fast as ye do this day, to make your voice to be heard on high. Is it such a fast that I have chosen? a day for a man to afflict his soul? is it to bow down his head as a bulrush, and to spread sackcloth and ashes under him? wilt thou call this a fast, and an acceptable day to the LORD? Is not this the fast that I have chosen? to loose the bands of wickedness, to undo the heavy burdens, and to let the oppressed go free, and that ye break every yoke?"

(Isaiah 58:4-6 KJV)

"This book of the law shall not depart out of thy mouth; but thou shalt meditate therein day and night, that thou mayest observe to do according to all that is written therein: for then thou shalt make thy way prosperous, and then thou shalt have good success."

(Joshua 1:8 KJV)

Saints are receiving songs from Heaven and ministering with the angels to bring great deliverance. Saints of God are visiting Heaven and learning how to transport body parts from Heaven to Earth. God is sending inventions down from Heaven to aid us in causing Earth's transfiguration to conform to Heaven. This is certainly the day where Jesus' prophesy is being fulfilled, and we are doing greater works than He did. This is the day of the fulfillment of Jesus' prayer when He prayed to the Father to permit Earth to be as it is in Heaven, for all evidence tells us that it won't be long. The saints of God are preparing the church for Jesus' return, and when He comes, His beloved . . . His bride will be without spot and without blemish, meaning that we will be perfect in all ways, physically, mentally, socially, economically, and otherwise. An example of a heartfelt cry from God is the following: *"Beloved, I pray that you may prosper in all things and be in health, just as your soul prospers,"* (3 John 1:2 NKJV). Healing today is a precursor to divine health.

Know, simply, that those who stagger at God's Word or those who trivialize God's Word are not the "disciples indeed". They are not among this end-time generation of saints, whom God has equipped and is equipping and sending into all the world to proclaim the Gospel. The seventy disciples who turned away from Jesus after witnessing the signs following His Name were not true disciples. When Jesus said in Mark 16:17 that the signs shall follow them who believe, the words "shall follow" in the Greek is parakoloutheo (para-kolou-theo, Strong's 3877), and it means to follow faithfully, to always be at one's side, to follow so closely in mind as to aspire to attain to the knowledge of it, and to conform one's self to it. No true follower of Christ, as Jesus defines follower, would ever turn back into the world, for to do so would be as a dog (man with an impure mind) going back to his own vomit, or a pig, having been washed, back to wallowing in the mud (see 2 Peter 2:22). If you hang around staggering or lukewarm Christians, find a new group to hang out with. If you cannot locate the kind of followers as defined by Jesus, why not go for the gold and experience the uninterrupted, incorruptible excellence of His power by depending totally on the Holy Ghost?

John 5:7 says that the Father, the Word, the Holy Spirit are all one person. When we trust God's Word, we are trusting God the Son. When we trust Jesus, we are trusting God. When we trust the Holy Spirit, we are trusting God. The Holy Spirit has been assigned to serve as our Earth-agent so that we are able to call upon Him for anything at any given moment. After all, it is Christ in us, the hope of glory. His glory reigns through us when we find unseen substances through our faith walk, thus, manifesting that expected end, which is our hope. Why do you suppose God told us to commit our works to Him so that He could establish our thoughts (Proverbs 16:3)? He wants us to think according to His Word so that His glory will be manifested. Why do you suppose God told us to trust in Him with all our hearts, minds, and souls and not to depend on our own understanding (Proverbs 3:5)? It is so that He could instruct us and tell us which way to go, because He wants to teach us (Psalm 32:8), He wants to lead us, He wants to protect us, and He wants to manifest Himself through us:

> *"And the glory which thou gavest me I have given them; that they may be one, even as we are one: I in them, and thou in me, that they may be made perfect in one; and that the world may know that thou hast sent me, and hast loved them, as thou hast loved me. Father, I will that they also, whom thou hast given me, be with me where I am; that they may behold my glory, which thou hast given me: for thou lovedst me before the foundation of the world."*
>
> (John 17:22-24 KJV)

God wants to have first place in our lives, and it is essential that we put first things first. After all, He is the Alpha . . .

Chapter Three

TRAPPED

"Woe to those who go down to Egypt for help, who rely on horses and trust in chariots because they are many and horsemen because they are very strong (influential people with titles), but they look not to the Holy One of Israel, nor seek and consult the Lord!"

(Isaiah 31:2 AMP)

Imagine yourself in this situation:

The day begins dandily. You've had so many of these lately; just go ahead and pinch yourself. Wife happy, children in college, except for the 16-year old, and if the past is any indication of the future, this next year and a half will shoot past like lightening. Aaaahhhh, just one more turn around the corner, and you and your wife will have the house all to yourselves, again. The job's going well, too. Thank God because your pastor frequently invites financial experts to conduct workshops giving practical financial advice, and with a praying wife to boot, there are no more money problems. That one didn't come easily. There were some critically painful adjustments in your spending practices, as recent as twelve years back, but, oh, how glad you are that you listened. And, best of all, eight more years, and you can throw away the clocks and calendars because everyday will be Sunday and a holiday. Yep! That's how you've always spelled retirement. What could be better?

To prevent having an interrupted evening, particularly since it's Friday, you take an extended lunch break in order to keep an appointment at the doctor's office for your semi-annual checkup. It was supposed to have been quick and routine, but not this one. This visit resulted in your returning home with a satchel full of prescription drugs, all lethal if you research the side effects, and a cloud of oppression cloaked between your skull and your brain. How did this happen? You felt just fine before leaving home. The receptionist was friendly enough. The office, however, was packed to capacity, one more patient and standing room only. That was enough to make you a bit irritable, but you seemed contained, at least to yourself, anyway. After sitting for forty-five minutes, your name is called. You are still contained — you think. The nurse shows you to a tiny little cubicle, just large enough for two small-to-medium-sized people to sit, period. The examining table stretched down the middle of the tiny floor suggests that it has been waiting there all along just for you, and satan's emissary begins his assignment: *Lord help me; I'm going to be sick.* Notice how you are thinking: He makes you personalize it. Spirit of infirmity, he's called, caressing your mind, and you accommodate him by mulling these thoughts over and over, rather than enforcing God's Word. You have forgotten that God commands you to control your thoughts. *"Casting down arguments and every high thing that exalts itself against the knowledge of God, bringing every thought into captivity to the obedience of Christ,"* (2 Corinthians 10:5 NKJV). The nurse takes your temperature and blood pressure and then goes out the door. Prior to closing you in, you see her tuck your chart into the plastic holder affixed to the door, flip the sign to "Occupied", and then poke her head slightly back inside, leaving you with the image of her bewitched smile before sealing you in. Now there is another thirty to forty minute wait. About this time, you are getting a bit antsy. You think, *They're talking about my case. I feel faint. Something is wrong with me. I knew I should have made an appointment last month.* The demon gains a bit more ground, by using you to focus your mind on the worst possible scenario

. . . pain, sickness, death, loneliness. All of these thoughts flash through your mind, and the sad part about it is, you receive and accept them as your very own.

You check your watch and realize you've waited an hour and forty-five minutes. An understanding boss is one thing, but the work still has to be done, and you had not planned to work late to catch up, especially on a Friday. Nor do you want to get to work early on Monday. After two days off, that "wisha-woulda" syndrome sets in, and it's a struggle just to mope through that early Monday's blues and clock in on time.

Finally, in storms the doctor, thrusting the door open, causing a strong breeze to clout the dusty air. He hurls the tail of his white jacket back as he steps to sit on the taller stool. These commanding motions, alone, are enough to intimidate you. "Looks like your pressure is up, 135/80. That's a bit high. You feel pretty drained, don't you?" It's called "suggestive destruction". How are you supposed to feel? A nearly two-hour wait is certain to drain anybody . . . anybody with the slightest bit of goings-on in his life. Just the mental challenge has stirred up emotions, causing the pressure to fluctuate. No one's blood pressure remains constant under stressful situations, but you don't think of that at this moment because you are overwrought. "Let me take your pressure again." His already grim expression becomes more dismal. *Oh, my God, it's bad news.* Fear escalates, and an old infirmity gains another notch. You are feeling warm. When the stethoscope is tightly wrapped around your arm, you can hear the palpitations, pulsating underneath your vest. The doctor pumps the bulb again and again, until the flesh is practically squeezed off your poor arm. *Whew!* He releases the little button on the pump, and the ball deflates. Tiny beads of sweat pop through the pores of your forehead. You both watch as the needle bobs on the instrument. He shakes his head slowly as he removes the band from your arm. *Gotcha!* That's the voice of that little demon which satan has assigned to you.

"She must have read it wrong," he whispers, pretending he doesn't want you to hear. The grim look returns with more intensity. "What or who in the world is troubling you? We're going to play this one safe. It's too high for you to leave here without taking something to bring it down. If you leave here today without medication, you may have a stroke or heart attack."

There goes my retirement. I may not live to see the girls graduate, let alone my son. I'll probably have a stroke or heart attack before I even retire. Demon on assignment, and you are listening. And, while you are listening to the demon, you are watching the doctor write prescription after prescription all the while he's talking. One, two, three, scribble, scribble, scribble.

Have you forgotten Proverbs 23:7 (KJV)? *"For as he [a man] thinketh in his heart, so is he."* Did you know that there is absolutely nothing the devil can do to you? The fact is, satan is powerless. He is not the lion he pretends to be, and he can only perform if given permission.

> *"They that see thee shall narrowly look upon thee, and consider thee, saying, Is this the man that made the earth to tremble, that did shake kingdoms?"*
> (Isaiah 14:16 KJV)

The day will come when those of the world will be so disappointed to learn that satan's influence was superficial from the beginning, and all that he presented before them was worthless. For one to follow satan only shows the corroding of his own power. The world's system is designed to oppose God and to operate without His guidance. No Christian has any place in the world, and satan's aim is to withdraw him from God's presence and blessings. The nature of a born-again Christian is to love God. How can one claim to love God and at the same time reject the guidance of the one he claims to love? How can a true Christian refuse to be under the authority of God and accept the authority of a proven liar? The only power satan has is that which you give to him, and he can only operate in your life with your permission. This includes sickness! Notice how these tiny imps coerce you into talking to yourself. Not only do they have you feeding yourself toxic information, but because you have not renewed your mind in God's Word, you are spiritually weak. This poisonous information is transmitted throughout your body and now taking a toll. We are living in a world today that is so filled with deception and corruption that we cannot, for a flicking moment, afford to drop our guard. The chief demon, satan, has programmed his emissaries to dictate to you how you feel, and you grab the bait, all the while thinking that you are the originator of these thoughts. It's satan's most effective trick!

"Yes, sir, doctor," no questions asked. Out you go to the next door, wagging your tail behind you, with two thoughts: one, the doctor says you are doomed and you must get the medication, and, two, do it! Yet, prior to going to the doctor's office, you felt just fine . . . great, as a matter of fact.

Whatever the doctor says, you do it. After all, he's the doctor, and his word is final authority. Lying demons shoot again.

WRONG! You're hooked! You're trapped! You have been duped! Have you forgotten that you are a Christian, a peculiar people, an ambassador in this land, subject only to Kingdom authority? The final authority in your world is God's Word and God's Word in your mouth brings you victory!

Is your doctor saved? Did you ask him? Does your doctor believe that God is a healer? Does your doctor believe that the leaves of the trees are for the healing of God's people?

"In the midst of the street of it, and on either side of the river, was there the tree of life, which bare twelve manner of fruits, and yielded her fruit every month: and the leaves of the tree were for the healing of the nations."
(Revelation 22:2 KJV)

Did you consult God prior to going to this doctor? *"In the thirty-ninth year of his reign Asa was diseased in his feet--until his disease became very severe; yet in his disease he did not seek the Lord, but relied on the physicians. And Asa slept with his fathers, dying in the forty-first year of his reign,"* (2 Chronicles 16:12, 13). And what about you? Do you believe that Christ Jesus paid for all sicknesses and diseases when He shed His Blood for you? Do you believe that God wants your body perfect, without spot and without blemish? Do you believe that you have the same genetic makeup inside your body as Christ Jesus? Do you believe that you have God's DNA? Too many questions — too few answers.

> *"Woe to those who go down to Egypt for help, who rely on horses and trust in chariots because they are many and horsemen because they are very strong [influential people], but they look not to the Holy One of Israel, nor seek and consult the Lord!"*
>
> (Isaiah 31:1 AMP, note added)

Chapter Four

WHO'S LEADING YOUR HEAD?

The body is always governed by the head

One of satan's key weapons is the weapon of fear, and sadly many of us have been taught that fear is normal. Let us resolve one crucial truth. Fear (Strong's 5832, Gk phobou) in any form of any type or nature is absolutely *not* normal, and it is horror and trepidation sent to you by satan himself!

All fear (as well as any of satan's other assaults) begins in the mind. Oftentimes, a misguided imagination causes one to think irrationally, and fear is introduced. When a person is ignorant of facts and has poor understanding of certain matters, confusion brings disruption in the psychological patterns of thinking, and fear sets in. The healthy imagination is shattered with unreasonable thought patterns, and the inability to rationalize opens the door to fear. Simply put, fears are perverted thoughts.

FEARS ARE PERVERTED THOUGHTS.

But, it's up to you as to how you handle or control your thoughts. Demon satan knows that if he can get into your head and control it, he can control your whole body, for the body is always governed by the head. John Milton writes in *Paradise Lost* (1667) that the mind is its own place and can make a Hell of Heaven, or a Heaven of Hell, as satan departs. Whoever controls the head is in control, no matter who the person is or what entity is being led. Any body, agency, corporation, institution, or group is always led by its head, and where the head directs, the body is compelled to follow.

Yet the Bible clearly tells us that God not only gives us the spirit of love and the spirit of power, but also the spirit of a sound mind.

> *"For God hath not given us the spirit of fear; but of power, and of love, and of a sound mind."*
> (2 Timothy 1:7 KJV)

When our minds are sound, we have total control of our thinking, meaning that we are fully in command of the thoughts we select to funnel through our brain and how we choose to act and react to those thoughts which we have permitted entrance. A sound mind is a trained, disciplined, healthy mind, and it is controlled by love, power, and healthy eating. It's no wonder God reminds us, *"There is no fear in love; but perfect love casts out fear, because fear involves torment. But he who fears has not been made perfect in love."* (1 John 4:18 NKJV)

If you have been a Christian for more than three months, and you've begun training in a good Bible-teaching church, one of the very first lessons you learned is taken from Romans 12:1-2 (KJV): *"I beseech you therefore, brethren, by the mercies of God, that you present your bodies a living sacrifice, holy and acceptable unto God, which is your reasonable service. And be not conformed to this world: but be ye transformed by the renewing of your mind, that ye may prove what is that good, and acceptable, and perfect, will of God."*

If we are to prove the good, acceptable, and perfect will of God for our lives, as well as for Kingdom profit, we must connect with the source. Our thinking must line up with God's thinking, for God desires that we have the mind of Christ.

> *"For who hath know the mind of the Lord, that he may instruct him? But we have the mind of Christ."*
> (1 Corinthians 2:16 KJV)

God doesn't simply command us to perform according to His rules, but He gives us great incentives for following them. When we allow our minds to follow the rules of God, we become fully persuaded that God is Who He says He is, and that He rewards those of us who diligently seek Him:

> *"But without faith it is impossible to please him: for he that cometh to God must believe that he is, and that he is a rewarder of them that diligently seek him."*
>
> (Hebrews 11:6 KJV)

Matthew 6:33 commands us to seek first the Kingdom of God, and when we do, many things, one after another, will be *added* to our lives.

> *"But seek ye first the kingdom of God, and his righteousness; and all these things shall be added unto you."*
>
> (Matthew 6:33 KJV)

How often have we heard of God's children suffering with infirmities, tricked into sickness, but after laboring in God's Word day in and day out, year in and year out, the infirmity disappears?

Taking Authority

For decades, I watched the renowned Evangelist/Pastor Benny Hinn humble himself and take up his cross daily to obey the voice of the Lord. Pastor Benny Hinn, as you probably know, is among today's top generals in the body of Christ, and he is just as strong today as he was over two decades ago when I first began watching him. A true evangelist, such as Pastor Hinn, will operate in the gift of faith. The gift of faith is different from the type of faith the Apostle Paul describes in Romans 12:3 (KJV): *"For I say through the grace given unto me, to every man that is among you, not to think of himself more highly than he ought to think; but to think soberly, accordingly as God has dealt to every man the measure of faith."* The type of faith the Apostle Paul mentions here is God's spiritual receptor, implanted into our spirits at the time of salvation, enabling us to receive spiritual revelation from the Holy Spirit. When we are born again, God, through the Holy Spirit, places His Spirit into our spirit, making us new creatures in Christ Jesus. At this very second, we are able to receive rhema — the revelatory knowledge of God's precious Word. When we read the Bible, the Spirit of Might is able to work within us, transforming us into the image of God. As we read the Word of God, the Spirit of Might engages Himself with our new spirit man, developing our spirit just as a fitness trainer develops his muscles. Just as the fitness trainer exercises his muscles to increase, strengthen, form, and define his body, our spirit man must be strengthened, developed, formed, and defined to exhibit the character of God. The more the trainer exercises, the stronger he gets and the more pronounced his muscles grow. This same process is necessary for the development of the spirit man: the more a convert reads the Word of God, the more the Spirit of Might causes the inner man to grow into the likeness of God. This is why Paul writes in Ephesians 3:16 (KJV), *"That he would grant you, according to the riches of His glory, to be strengthened with might by His Spirit in the inner man;"* This would explain why some men would have little faith (Matthew 6:30, 8:26, 14:31, 16:8), and some, great faith (Matthew 8:10, 15:28, Luke 7:9, Acts 6:8). The Bible also speaks of shipwrecked faith, childlike faith, and more. The point I am making is this: Your level of faith depends on the level of God's Word implanted into your spirit and the degree to which you will accept the truth of God's Word. Accepting the truth of God's Word assures us that our faith will not be shipwrecked. To play it safe, and to avoid deception, position your mind to accept the fullness of God's Word. In doing so, you are positioning yourself to make changes. God's Word comes to rebuke, correct, and instruct us for our own good (2 Timothy 3:16), and in order for us to conform to God's Word, we must make adjustments in our lives if we are to please Him.

If our faith is to please God, then we must align our hearts with His Word. Notice in Romans 12:3, when the Holy Spirit breathed upon Paul to write this sentence, He did not say that God gave to each man 'a' measure of faith. If that were the case, at the time of conversion, God could have given one man a sliver of faith and another an ocean full of faith, each 'a' measure of faith, but different sizes, thus, making Him a respecter of persons — a God who displays partiality. But this is certainly not the case, for God is no respecter of persons. God is, however, a respecter of faith because faith is what puts into motion every single plan of action that ever was, is, or is to come. Faith is what created the world and everything in it, including you and me. Thus, because we were created by faith, God deems it natural that we should live by the evidence from which we were produced.

> "Now faith is the substance of things hoped for, the evidence of things not seen."
>
> (Hebrews 11:1 KJV)

BECAUSE WE WERE CREATED BY FAITH, GOD DEEMS IT FITTING THAT WE SHOULD LIVE BY THE EVIDENCE FROM WHICH WE WERE PRODUCED

But, the gift of faith is one of the gifts which operates, not exclusively, but predominately under an evangelical gift, and it accompanies miracles. Well, certainly, Pastor Benny Hinn fits perfectly into this mold. In fact, I believe that without disputation, he could easily be labeled the "Miracle Man". Wherever he goes, signs, wonders, and miracles follow, just as they did some twenty or so years ago. I feel it safe to say that Pastor Benny Hinn set a new standard for the healing ministry of this era. Healing had become Benny Hinn's signature, and all over the world, testimonials flow regarding the supernatural healings his followers are enjoying. Countless life-sentencing diseases are reported healed at his meetings, both at home and abroad.

But Benny Hinn was infirmed. That's right. During all those years of preaching and teaching the Word of God and seeing probably hundreds of thousands, or even millions, healed as the result of God's anointing working through him, Pastor Benny Hinn, himself, was infirmed! I don't recall the exact year, but somewhere between 2004 and 2006, right here in Jacksonville, Florida, at his very own crusade, God healed Benny Hinn of the infirmity that he had carried in his body for decades.

Everything we read in the Bible either has happened or will happen. What is written is written so that we are made believers. *"These things have I written unto you that believe on the name of the Son of God; that ye may know that ye have eternal life, and that ye may believe on the name of the Son of God,"* (1 John 5:13 KJV). There is a time in the Bible when Jesus had to speak more than one time before the blind man received his sight:

> *"And he cometh to Bethsaida; and they bring a blind man unto him, and besought him to touch him. And he took the blind man by the hand, and led him out of the town; and when he had spit on his eyes, and put his hands upon him, he asked him if he saw ought. And he looked up, and said, I see men as trees, walking. After that he put his hands again upon his eyes, and made him look up: and he was restored, and saw every man clearly."*
> (Mark 8:22-25 KJV)

Most of the times, Jesus only spoke a word — gave a command — and the healing was manifested. This is a miracle. Healing is progressive. Miracles are God's supernatural intervention, and they happen instantly. Now you see it — now you don't. The sickness or disease is here, and then it's gone.

Through his acclaim, through his strong faith in healing for others, Benny Hinn is no different than most of us. We believe in healing for others, but when it comes to our own healing, a roadblock emerges. Recently I heard a renown pastor state that the healing power God gives us is for others and not for ourselves. Based on my own experience, I cannot subscribe to this theory because I have laid hands on myself many times and haved received healing. I have also heard many ministers testify that they were given life-threatening diagnosis and after shutting themselves off from the world for a day or two and fasting and praying and laying hands on themselves, the sickness left. Most of us have positioned ourselves to receive healing for others but have built road blocks for ourselves which have inhibited us from receiving healing for ourselves. Healing is there. It was given to us at Calvary. Shortly after the Apostle Paul reveals our identity to us in the Book of Romans by making us aware that we are new creatures in Christ Jesus and all of our old ways have been washed under the Blood, He tells us to renew our minds. Unless we adopt a new mindset, we will remain in bondage . . . a hidden treasure buried by the strains and corruption of the world system. If we don't allow our minds to be renewed, and if we don't allow the Holy Spirit to breathe upon our thought processes, then we will never permit the mind of Christ to surface in our lives.

But what happens when a saint's mind is renewed and the spirit of infirmity wants to assert its presence? This brings to mind the story of Dorothy and Little Ricky. Dorothy is a very precious, uncompromising Christian I know who lives here in Jacksonville, Florida. Her full name is Dorothy Roberts, and she has written a book called *A Walk Through Tears*. If ever you want to be encouraged, you should purchase this uplifting book. As the story goes, Dorothy's son, Ricky, was born mentally deformed with no mental capacity for learning. Morning, noon, and night, at every opportunity, Dorothy prayed for her child. Whenever Dorothy heard of an anointed prayer meeting, near or far, she and Little Ricky were there. Oftentimes, she traveled hundreds of miles, just to have an anointed minister lay hands on Little Ricky. On the surface, things seemed to worsen, but Dorothy had a renewed mind, and she lived out 2 Corinthians 5:7 (KJV): *"For we walk by faith, not by sight."* At one point during her many struggles, the principal of Little Ricky's school called Dorothy in for a conference and asked her to remove Ricky from the school and institutionalize her baby, but praise God, Dorothy trusted God's Word as opposed to yielding her mind to the voice of satan. Today, little Ricky is an accomplished minister of the Gospel of Christ Jesus, holding, not two, not three, but five or six PhD's! And, it is all because his mother, Dorothy, resisted satan's invitations to give up on her child! She refused to walk in fear and intimidation, and she sought the power of God whenever, wherever, and through whomever she could find it.

Once we accept the fact that God really did create us to reign as kings and priests, and that He knows more than we know — not just about ourselves, but about everything in this entire world, including all that pertains to us, to position us into the role of our heavenly calling — it becomes a delight to pursue Him with all of our hearts, knowing that His plan for our lives far exceeds anything we can possibly imagine, and certainly far exceeds that which we have conjured up. It is at this point we are able to connect our minds to the mind of Christ through His Word. We are now able to *". . . let this mind be in [us] which was also in Christ Jesus, who, being in the form of God, thought it not robbery to be equal with God,"* (Philippians 2:5-6 KJV). It is at this point we begin to move fearlessly in God's power and wisdom, forsaking the deeds of the flesh and triumphing over life's challenges. Dorothy is a wonderful example. Today, while her son Ricky oversees the

True Light Ministries in Jacksonville, plus several other cities in the states of Florida and Georgia, Dorothy is his administrator, fulfilling the call of God in her life, which was birthed through her steadfast stand for her son's healing.

Plant it firmly in your brain that satan's entry into our affairs comes only through the mind, and one of his primary cohorts is fear. Yet, 2 Timothy 1:7 (NKJV) says, *"For God has not given us a spirit of fear, but of power and of love and of a sound mind."* Fear masquerades with many coverings, among which are sorrow, dread, self-pity, worry, anxiety, nervousness, confusion, dismay, heaviness, rejection, unhappiness, loneliness, and so forth; and all of these mental attitudes are satanic attacks on the mind. These states of beings are electives, and you have a choice. In Dorothy's case, among other forms of fear, I can imagine that rejection scored highest. Imagine the little children on the playground treating her son as though he was some sort of monster. Imagine the principal, of all people, advising her to dehumanize and institutionalize the child. I could go on, but I believe rejection ran rampant through Dorothy's family on a daily basis. Was there sorrow? Probably. But Dorothy knew to put on the garment of praise for the spirit of heaviness (Isaiah 61:3). Fear, in masses, knocked on Dorothy's door, but Dorothy kept them out by trusting the Word of God with her heart (Proverbs 3:5). Trusting God's Word demands direct application.

God admonishes us in Deuteronomy 30:19, *"I call heaven and earth to record this day against you, that I have set before you life and death, blessing and cursing; therefore choose life, that both thou and thy seed may live."* I find it interesting here that God would set before us life first and then death. At this juncture, God most likely means spiritual life, because He follows by inferring that spiritual life will reap blessing and spiritual death will reap cursing. These blessings or cursings will not only be manifest in your life but also in the lives of your seed. I believe if God had meant physical life or death that He would have excluded the seed, because reproduction ceases at the time of physical death.

On the other hand, Proverbs 18:21 (KJV) reads, *"Death and life are in the power of the tongue: and they that love it shall eat the fruit thereof."* Here, the Holy Spirit is at work, making careful observations as to how mankind has applied God's Promises; for now, King Solomon is instructed to acknowledge that man has chosen death over life. In doing so, Solomon writes exactly what the Holy Spirit tells him to record. God looked down on His Creation, and through the words coming from man's voice, He listened to the disparaging choices man made about his life and himself, century after century. He watched as man drifted further and further away from Him, and how the language of man appeased flesh, conforming to worldly circumstances rather than to appeasing God and conforming to God's Word. He listened to man respond to his feelings by taking a solid verbal stand on what and how he felt: it was the voice of man's choice, notwithstanding the fact that God had made his instruction so simple that a newborn child could not miss it. He said, "Choose life!"

I believe the Holy Spirit was enraged when He dictated Proverbs 18:21 to King Solomon. Notice, He warned us of death first: "Death" is in the power of your tongue, and you seem to love death more than you love life! I did not set before you death and life, but I set before you life, then death. Death was the latter. I'm warning you, you choose death, and you will suffer the consequences! If you choose life, you will enjoy its fruit! Choose life and live! Stop choosing death!

Can't you hear him? He associates the outcome of your words of obedience with fruit, symbolizing that health is eminent when you choose life. Choosing life relegates love, joy, peace, long suffering, gentleness, goodness, faith, meekness, temperance — fruit.

Notice the Scripture before, in Proverbs 18:20 (KJV): *"A man's belly shall be satisfied with the fruit of his mouth; and with the increase of his lips shall he be filled."* The Message translation of these two Scriptures read, *"Words satisfy the mind as much as fruit does the stomach; good talk is as gratifying as a good harvest. Words kill, words give life, they're either poison or fruit - you choose."* Choose to embrace or to love life, and when you do, you will eat and bear in your body and in your life its bountiful harvest.

Almost daily, I am reminded of a statement written at the beginning of Dr. Charles Capps' little handbook on confessions where he mentions that God spoke to him and said, "I told my people to say what they want, and my people are saying what they have." The Holy Spirit had the Apostle Paul write it this way, ". . . [call] those things which be not as though they were," (Romans 4:17 KJV). Were is a past tense. In other words, our place of expectancy should rest in the evidence of things not seen. We are to know that what we want from God has already been supplied, and that includes healing. When it comes to healing, God specifically tells us that we have it already. Once we grasp the full meaning of Isaiah 53:4-5, we will always see ourselves perfectly healed. *"Surely He has borne our griefs (sicknesses, weaknesses, and distresses) and carried our sorrows and pains [of punishment], yet we [ignorantly] considered Him stricken, smitten and afflicted by God [as if with leprosy]. But He was wounded for our transgressions, He was bruised for our guilt and iniquities; the chastisement [needful to obtain] peace and well-being for us was upon Him, and with the stripes [that wounded] Him we are healed and made whole,"* (Isaiah 53:4-5 AMP). Healing has already been provided. Simply receive what belongs to you.

Love Blasts Fear to Smithereens!

Just as prayer is the least-attended church activity in the body of Christ, but the most powerful weapon God has given us to defeat the devil, love is the most loosely implemented and trivialized inheritance among the gifts. Yet love is the greatest of all the gifts.

> *"And now abide faith, hope, love, these three; but the greatest of these is love."*
> (1 Corinthians 13:13 NKJV)

Wake up, saints! Why do you think the devil does not want you to attend prayer meetings? Why do you think satan will plant his allies of persecution wherever you are, when you make up your mind that you are going to pray, and especially when you begin praying in tongues? Because he has no recourse, that's why! Demon satan realizes that if you pray, he's defeated, and the burning inferno is all that remains for him.

In like manner, why do you suppose that whenever the pastor teaches on love, your mind droops to a boring, *Yeah, yeah, I know how to love,* and that's the end of the story? That very same Sunday, you leave the church, eyeballing Gossiping Gertrude, the one you call 'Sister Know-it-all' because the pastor appointed her to oversee the children's ministry, instead of your best friend. You proceed to go about your own way, loving those who love you, and as for the others, well… You've fallen victim to another one of satan's tricks. He realizes that if you purpose in your heart to truly walk in love, he has no power over you, nor does he have power over your enemies, because love will make your enemies be at peace with you and sometimes love you in return. God cannot be pleased without faith (Hebrews 11:6), yet faith will not work except that it works by love.

> *"For in Jesus Christ neither circumcision availeth any thing, nor uncircumcision; but faith which worketh by love."*
> (Galatians 5:6 KJV)

Love is the most powerful gift we have, not only to conquer satan, but also to win others to Christ, because pure love all but blinds us to the faults of others.

*"And above all things have fervent love for one another,
for 'love will cover a multitude of sins'."*
(1 Peter 4:8 NKJV)

Love not only hides a multitude of sins, but perfect love casts out fear (1 John 4:18). In a fraction of a second, fear literally shudders, shatters, disintegrates, and disappears in the eyes of perfect love. Fear is absolutely annihilated and blown to smithereens!

According to Dr. Caroline Leaf's book *Who Switched Off My Brain*, fear triggers more than 1,400 known physical and chemical responses created by negative thoughts, and this activates more than 30 different hormones and neurotransmitters combined, throwing the body into a frantic state of being (pp 36-37). But sickness can neither enter nor remain in a body that houses a mind governed by perfect love. Perfect love not only casts out fear, but it also brings forth healing when God's Word is appropriated.

I recall an incident I experienced during my stay in Indiana. God had once again relocated me, and I was just settling into my God-given miracle house. The Lord had sent me from California to Indiana, where most of my immediate family lives. I had no money and no place to stay, but because of a very close-knit, loving family, my oldest brother welcomed me into his home. I didn't know my brother was on drugs until I moved in. However, the move was clearly orchestrated by God, because my brother was set free once satan was exposed, and I broke his strongholds through intercession. That's another wonderful story, which I hope to share at another time.

An important point to remember is that where God directs, He always provides. After three months with my brother, time enough to clean house, so to speak, it was time for me to move, and I went house shopping. That's right! I had no job and no money, but I set out to find a starter home since it was just me. Wouldn't you know it, my mother learned that I was house shopping, and she gave me a seven-room house, land, title, and the whole deal!

This was truly a miracle from God! The house needed a bit of work, but I didn't mind the work because I saw where I could add an additional bathroom and bedroom upstairs.

Once the work was done I was ready for a larger home, so I decided to rent that house and purchase another one. Still, no job and no money. I dressed immaculately, got my leather briefcase with brown leather heels to match, put on my sophisticated caramel and white checkered suit with a white, cashmere turtleneck sweater to set it off. Stepping high, I entered the realtor's office. They were impressed with me, and I was impressed that they were impressed. The realtor worked extremely hard for me, calling me to look at properties on a daily basis. It wasn't long before he got a feel for my requirements, and within two weeks, we had the perfect house. Although I was excited when I saw the building, I didn't let him see me gloating. The neighborhood wasn't that great, but I knew that would change once I moved in. As I stated earlier, light always extinguishes darkness, provided it is turned on. In a very professional manner, I expressed my sincere interest and told the realtor to draw up the contract. With much excitement, he followed through, and the next day he presented the contract to me for approval. I took the papers home and read them carefully. When I got to the price of the enormous figure — I can't exactly recall today, but I know it was far, far beyond One Hundred Thousand Dollars, a huge price to me at that time. I suppose I don't recall the price, because at first glance, my brain instantly rejected it. I slashed the figure and wrote Twenty Eight Thousand Dollars. The huge three-story brick complex had seven bathrooms and six bedrooms. Lovely woodwork throughout the building was solid birch, and it had a gorgeous wood-burning fireplace in the living room, with the most exquisite storage cabinets built into the walls on the second floor. The hardwood floors were almost like new, and I could see myself renting most of the bedrooms to boarders in order to pay the mortgage.

The next morning, I handed the realtor the executed contract. "Ma'am," he frowned, "you've got to be kidding." Mind you, this man had gotten on a first name basis with me, prior to seeing the Twenty-Eight Thousand Dollar figure. "Oh, no," I pleasantly smiled, "that's my price, Twenty Eight-Thousand Dollars." "I can't take this to them," he gruffed, "They'll think I'm crazy." He abruptly pushed the papers back my way. I gently glided the contract right back to him with a tender but authoritative smile. "The law says you have to." Those words came straight from the Holy Spirit. I knew absolutely nothing about real estate and its laws, and there was no way I could have so much as imagined what the law said. In fact, whatever legal rights I might have had did not enter my mind, even after I made the statement. It was the next day that I realized what I had said, and I called my lawyer-cousin to learn the impact.

When I was much younger, prior to my salvation, I would go to church just to hear the singing. Oh, I had gotten baptized at a very early age, but only Heaven knows what, if any, significance it held for me at the time. After the singing, my girlfriend and I would make it to the exit door. Before the singing, however, the Baptist church we attended had what we called a devotion service. During the devotion service, testimonials went forth, and practically each Sunday the same testimonials were given by the same parishioners. One of the statements many of those giving testimonials would say went something like this: *Lord, I praise you for protecting me from dangers, seen and unseen.* Being the heathens we were, my girlfriend and I often made fun of those heart-felt comments, having absolutely no revelation of what those precious old women were saying.

Today, however, it's a different story. While I may not always be in tune to how God is providing protection for me, I am always sure that He's there to keep me from evil of any sort. Dangers come in many forms, some through physical illness or physical harm, and others through mental, social, or financial harm. During this chapter in my life, God was not only providing supernatural financial provisions for me, but also He would show me the power He had given me over satan in health, ensuring divine protection. He would not allow satan to steal my blessings.

> *"And when they bring you unto the synagogues, and unto magistrates, and powers, take ye no thought how or what thing ye shall answer, or what ye shall say. For the Holy ghost shall teach you in the same hour what ye ought to say."*
>
> (Luke 12:11-12 KJV)

When we have a heart for God, we will certainly get an unction from Him, and He does teach us all things (1 John 2:20). The Holy Spirit will always tell you what to say at the appropriate time.

The next afternoon, the telephone rang. When I answered, the realtor started in with, "You won't believe this." I recognized his voice.

"Oh, yes I will," I replied, "They accepted the contract."

He replied, "They did, and I still can't believe it!" He was dumbfounded.

At the closing, I watched as papers were passed from one realtor to the other, and then to me for signature. You would have thought I was just as knowledgeable as the pros: cool, calm, and collected . . . and careful not to talk too much. Paper after paper, my realtor briefly identified each. I acted as if I knew exactly what he described, but I slightly glanced over each page as though for accuracy, and then I signed them, page by page.

Prior to going to the closing, I was penniless, but at the close of the meeting, the realtor handed me a check for Nine thousand Thirty Five Dollars. "Thank you," was my quiet and tender response, as though I was expecting the money, then, I unpretentiously slipped the check into my purse, after examining the name and the amount. The truth is, I wanted to leap and faint at the same time. To this day, I have no idea as to how the seller paid me Nine Thousand Thirty Five Dollars. I only know that it had to be a miracle from God.

The broker of the company was at the closing. My guess is that this entire deal was a mystery to them all. The boss, too, wanted to witness it to the very end. "I never saw anything like this in my life," the broker said again. The meeting had ended, and everyone was preparing to leave. This was about the fourth time I had heard those words in a matter of minutes. Finally, I relented and said, "Then you need to get to know the God I know."

While the incident I describe above does not describe a healing, it is a typical example of how God wants us to walk without fear and intimidation. Faith moves forward on trust when all circumstances dictate that failure is inevitable. Faith never considers the advantages of oppositions but only the Promises of God.

Drinking the Bleach

Moving into my lovely home, my first task was to sanitize the building. I had completed the upstairs, and the main floor was next. It was summertime, and there was no air conditioner, which brought on great thirsts, particularly since I was working hard to make the place look and smell brand new. I love water, and then as now, I drank it by the quarts, filling the old mayonnaise jar to the brim and keeping a jar by my side, something I saw my dad do when I was growing up.

The building extended about a hundred feet from front to back, which made it a long stretch, carrying cleaning supplies back and forth. The only running water in the front of the house was in the tiny guest lavatory, and drinking water was difficult to draw from this itty-bitty sink and pour into the pail. So, I loaded up with mop, rags, a pail of water, cleanser, disinfectant, and a quart of bleach, which I poured to the brim to keep from toting the full gallon and one half bottle to the front. A quart of bleach was not a lot, considering I had to clean the toilet, the face bowl, window sills, floors, etc. I was on a roll, and at least an hour had passed. I had also built up an unquenchable thirst, so when I rose from my knees, after cleaning the corners with a rag and toothbrush, I reached for the quart. All I could see was the jar of nice, cool water. I took the jar, and without thinking, turned the bottle up to my mouth. I did not let it down until the entire quart was guzzled up. When I released the jar from my mouth, I got my first whiff of the contents. Yikes! It was bleach! I had drunk the entire quart of bleach, and because I had been so thirsty, I had not realized it until after it was all gulped down.

Now, here's the key: Not once did I get upset or panic, but my mind swiftly went to Jesus. The story of Paul on the Melita island flashed through my mind.

> *"And when they were escaped, then they knew that the island was called Melita. And the barbarous people shewed us no little kindness; for they kindled a fire, and received us every one, because of the present rain, and because of the cold. And when Paul had gathered a bundle of sticks, and laid them on the fire, there came a viper out of the heat, and fastened on his hand and when the barbarians saw the venomous beast hang on his hand, they said among themselves, No doubt this man is a murderer, whom, though he hath escaped the sea, yet vengeance suffered not to live. And he shook off the beast into the fire, and felt no harm. Howbeit they looked when he should have swollen, or fallen down dead suddenly; but they had looked a great while, and saw no harm come to him, they changed their minds, and said that he was a god."*
>
> (Acts 28:1-6 KJV)

89

I looked at the jar in my hand and said, *"Oh, well, I shall drink any poisonous thing, and it shall not harm me."* I didn't run to call an ambulance or run to get some milk. In fact, as I recall the incident, I didn't even think about it again, until times such as this, when I wanted to help increase the faith of other Christians.

Years later, I visited a woman in Jacksonville, Florida, who had accidentally drunk a very small amount of bleach, two or three weeks before my visit. The dear old woman was still gasping for breath, taking every kind of medication and nutrient recommended. Yet, in spite of everything, she gagged and coughed, still showing strong evidence of chemical toxins remaining in her system. This lady was a Christian, but she had never learned the power of her mind and her words, which she inherited as the result of her new birth. She was never taught how to appropriate God's Word, making it come off the pages into her everyday situations. Faith was not a way of life for her. She had not been taught to inoculate her body against sickness with the Word of God. Consequently, fear had taken over, and ultimately she had become sick as a result of drinking the bleach. Had she walked in perfect love, the fear would have fled. The spirit of love will always torment fear and will also cause us to think thoughts of empowerment.

No Weapon Formed Against You Shall Prosper

God did not promise the weapons would not form. Demon satan will attempt to attack, but God promises that the weapons will not prosper. He is always there to protect us and raise up a standard against the enemy.

Next door to the house I had just purchased was a large vacant lot, which was a part of my title deed. I noticed immediately that wayward men, young and old, would gather on the lot, drinking, smoking, and conducting themselves with less than godly manners. Without delay or reservation, I went to the lot the very next time I saw the gathering and introduced myself, explaining that I was the new owner of the building, and I did not want them gathering outside to drink. I did tell them that I was a Christian, and if they wanted, they could come inside and drink cold drinks. After praying with several of the men, the crowd disbursed and did not return to the lot.

Two or three days later, I saw a long black Cadillac limousine pull up across the street, and three men got out and had begun walking up the stairs. It was clear that they lived a worldly life, and my guess is that they were drug dealers. I took my Bible, paraded across the street, stepped up a few of the stairs, caught up to them, and greeted them by saying, "Hello, gentlemen, my name is Lola, and I am a servant of the Most High God. Are you gentlemen saved?"

One quickly replied with a challenging tone, "My *daddy* is a preacher." To which I retorted with an overriding tone, "I didn't ask you about your daddy; I asked you about you. Are you saved?" Neither responded, but I proceeded with respect to witness to them. I ended by informing them that our street was being committed to God, and they would be welcome to attend Bible studies, which I would begin holding in my home. This was my sincere demonstration of love. What could they say, except "Thank you?"

I had not noticed the men taking furniture into the building, but the next day, I saw them loading furniture into a truck and vacating the building. Darkness can never remain when light appears. *"Let your light so shine before men, that they may see your good works, and glorify your Father which is in heaven,"* (Matthew 5:16 KJV). Purpose in your hearts that you will obey this command by allowing your light to shine, extinguishing all darkness in your space.

There was a liquor store on the corner, and it wasn't two months after I moved into the neighborhood that the store closed.

I awoke one morning and was going to water the grass when I noticed a strange symbol etched on my sidewalk, outside the front gate. I wasn't sure what it meant, but I knew it was a threat. Someone later told me that it was the mark of a gang, a threat that they were going to kill me. I simply pleaded the Blood of Jesus over the etching, as well as the entire street, and sent every message back to the sender in the Name of Jesus! Not once did I have a problem with the gangs. In fact, at every opportunity, I prayed for those I felt needed help, when I was fortunate to find one who did. Know this: Our street proved to be the safest and most attractive street in the neighborhood.

Saints of God, where are you? When God says He gives us power over all the works of the enemy (Luke 10:19), He means exactly what He says. Fear has torment, and many sicknesses dwell in the bodies of saints because they live a life of fear. If that's you, repent for dishonoring God's Word, and begin confessing today that God has not given you a spirit of fear but of power, of love, and of a sound mind. Say it over and over again, until it becomes a revelation to you. Only when you realize the authenticity of God's Word will you walk in complete wholeness and victory.

Chapter Five

TRAIN YOUR BRAIN

" . . . [love] thinks no evil . . ."
(1 Corinthians 13:5 NKJV)

Lethal Thinking vs. Godly Thinking

In addition to learning God's Ways and growing into that Father-child relationship, another reason God issues a command for us to study His Word is for us to be able to cleanse our minds of any debris and to free ourselves of "lethal thinking". Remember, Proverbs 23:6-7 warns us that we become what we think: *"Do not eat the bread of a miser, Nor desire his delicacies; For as he thinks in his heart, so is he."*

> Also, *"That he might sanctify and cleanse it with the washing of water by the Word."*
> (Ephesians 5:26 KJV)

What we think affects our entire body. The whole body is a composite of cells, and these cells contain branches of nerves similar to branches we see sprouting from the limbs of trees. Just as you give water to the tree to make it grow, you make the branches in your cells grow with the thoughts you process through your brain. These branches constantly grow throughout your entire body: in your brain, your arms, your legs, your stomach — all of you. Your thought-life is retained in these nerve cells in your body, and as you think, you release chemicals into these cells. Good thoughts result from both the left side of the brain and from

93

the right side of the brain working synergistically. In the past, we were led to believe that the left side of the brain processed academia and the right side of the brain was our creative side. We were taught that these two sides worked independently. Today, however, those theories have been dismissed. According to Dr. Caroline Leaf, the left side of the brain gives us details of the big picture and the right side of the brain gives us the big picture of the details. Thus, these two sides cooperate to fit perfectly together giving the brain a 2 + 2 = 4 on its right side, and a 4 = 2 + 2 on its left side. Synchronization is accomplished in the brain when our thinking is positive, and it releases good chemicals into every cell in the body, with the result of bringing about wellness. When one chooses to entertain evil thoughts, the brain becomes unbalanced, and then distorted electrical feedback turns into toxic chemicals in the brain. These lethal chemicals are released from the brain into the cells of the body, resulting in sickness. Good thoughts produce good chemicals in the body, which produce good health. Bad thoughts produce bad chemicals in the cells, which produce bad health. It is simply amazing how far modern science has come to finally parallel its studies with the Word of God. *"For as he thinks in his heart, so is he."* (Proverbs 23:7 NKJV)

You have the capacity to accept or reject both the good and the evil information presented. To prove to you the unlimited control you have over your brain, let's look at advertising, as an example. Consumer experts tell us that we literally come in contact with hundreds, even thousands, of advertisements daily: Internet, television, radio, billboards, books, newspapers, flyers, brochures, business cards, window posters, telephone marketers, supermarkets, etc. As each piece of new information is presented to the brain, the brain filters each message, retaining the ones it selects to keep and dismissing or tossing into the "abeyance file" the ones it chooses not to consider. Imagine the discarded information as the information you delete from your computer. The information is tossed into the "trash bin", but it doesn't permanently leave the computer. To allow ourselves to maintain a reasonable amount of daily focus, we sift much of the information presented before us out of our forethoughts and into that so-called "abeyance file" or "trash bin". Every piece of information flashing before your mind is introduced to your "thought process", and it is your decision as to whether you will accept it or reject it.

Everything you do begins with a thought. Thoughts produce emotions; emotions produce attitudes; attitudes produce behavior. If you choose to accept lethal thoughts, then processing these thoughts begin with your emotions. These evil, toxic thoughts are stored inside every cell in your body, and these thoughts are at work to produce within you the nature of what you have selected to think.

The good news is, YOUR THOUGHTS ARE CONTROLLABLE. As you revisit the "advertisement" example, you can readily see how much control you actually do have over your mind. Several books have been written about the battleground of the mind. Because the mind is a "battleground", war is forever ensuing, and this means that we must fight by using God's artillery!

"For though we walk in the flesh, we do not war according to the flesh. For the weapons of our warfare are not carnal but mighty in God for pulling down strongholds, casting down arguments and every high thing that exalts itself against the knowledge of God, bringing every thought into captivity to the obedience of Christ." (2 Corinthians 10:3-6 NKJV) The word "arguments" in the King James Version of the Bible is "imaginations". God is telling us to reject all evil thoughts introduced to our minds that disagree with or conflict with the Word of God.

Your mind and your brain are one and the same. The mind and body connection are real, which is why God says in Proverbs 23:7 that you become whatsoever you think. You may have been told by your doctor, "It's all in your head." What the doctor did not realize was that everything that results in your body is the result of your thought-life — what's in your head. So, in essence, the doctor was correct, notwithstanding the fact that he was subtly dismissing your condition. However, don't go blaming your doctor for a misdiagnosis, because he or she only alluded to what he or she has been taught. Only in recent years has the medical industry given serious attention to the study of the brain. Brain specialists such as Dr. Leaf have proven that the brain is the most important organ in the body and is designed to control the entire body. I believe that this is why God has instructed us: *"Thou shalt love the Lord thy God with all thy heart, and with all thy soul, and with all thy mind,"* (Matthew 22:37 KJV). When we view some of Strong's definitions of heart, soul, and mind, we get a more vivid picture of the extent to which God wants us to commit ourselves.

The Heart:
1) the heart
1a) that organ in the animal body which is the centre of the circulation of the blood, and hence was regarded as the seat of physical life
1b) denotes the centre of all physical and spiritual life
2a) the vigour and sense of physical life
2b) the centre and seat of spiritual life
2b1) the soul or mind, as it is the fountain and seat of the thoughts, passions, desires, appetites, affections, purposes, endeavors
2b2) of the understanding, the faculty and seat of the intelligence
2b3) of the will and character
2b4) of the soul so far as it is affected and stirred in a bad way or good, or of the soul as the seat of the sensibilities, affections, emotions, desires, appetites, passions
1c) of the middle or central or inmost part of anything, even though inanimate

The heart is the most vital organ in the body. If it stops, everything stops. When it operates properly, it causes life to stream throughout your body. This is the organ through which the blood flows, and the life of the flesh is in the blood. I find it interesting that whether a sickness is high blood pressure or drug addiction, the first organ satan weakens is the heart. Strengthening nutrients such as CoQ10, MCHA Calcium and Magnesium, Omega 3-6-9, L-Arginine, etc., are among the primary nutrients health practitioners recommend for heart strength.

". . . for the life of all flesh is the blood thereof . . ."
(Leviticus 17:14 KJV)

No heart — no blood. No blood — no life. No life — no flesh. Now you are able to see why God has instructed us, *"Thou shalt love the Lord thy God with all thy heart, and with all thy soul, and with all thy mind,"* (Matthew 22:37 KJV). When we love God with all our hearts (*Kardia* in Greek), we produce a flow or "fountain and seat of the thoughts, passions, desires, appetites, affections, purposes, endeavors," (Strong's G2588) which stream into our will and character. This causes God's will to become our will, and this causes His character to become reproduced through our character.

The Soul:
1) breath
1a) the breath of life
1a1) the vital force which animates the body and shows itself in breathing
1a1a) of animals
1a12) of men
1b) life
1c) that in which there is life
1c1) a living being, a living soul
2) the soul
2a) the seat of the feelings, desires, affections, aversions (our heart, soul etc.)

97

2b) the (human) soul in so far as it is constituted that by the right use of the aids offered it by God it can attain its highest end and secure eternal blessedness, the soul regarded as a moral being designed for everlasting life

2c) the soul as an essence which differs from the body and is not dissolved by death (distinguished from other parts of the body) (Strong's G5590)

When loving God with all of our hearts is being exercised, an understanding is created in our souls which controls the very breath we breathe. We become conscious of inhaling and exhaling. We cherish the Spirit of God flowing through our spirits and causing us to take command of any words projecting from our lips, for we realize that we are "living souls" or talking spirits. We intentionally become definitive in what we create.

> *"A wholesome tongue is a tree of life, But perverseness in it breaks the spirit."*
>
> (Proverbs 15:4 NKJV)

The Mind:

1) the mind as a faculty of understanding, feeling, desiring
2) understanding
3) mind, i.e. spirit, way of thinking and feeling
4) thoughts, either good or bad (Strong's)

Through deliberate implementation of the love of God in our hearts and souls, we now recognize, differentiate, and distribute information introduced to our minds — embracing the good and dismissing the evil. Our minds are now "stayed on God" so that we are now able to enjoy His perfect peace.

> *"Thou wilt keep him in perfect peace, whose mind is stayed on thee: because he trusteth in thee."*
>
> (Isaiah 26:3 KJV)

We now have the same mind as Christ because we "let" or "allow" our minds think His thoughts. God is not an unreasonable God. When He tells us to "let", He is issuing a command, and He would never issue a command to us without first training us to perform. His instructions are clearly written in the training manual:

"I beseech you therefore, brethren, by the mercies of God, that you present your bodies a living sacrifice, holy, acceptable to God, which is your reasonable service. And do not be conformed to this world, but be transformed by the renewing of your mind, that you may prove what is that good and acceptable and perfect will of God."
(Romans 12:1-2)

"Let this mind be in you, which was also in Christ Jesus: Who, being in the form of God, thought it not robbery to be equal with God: But made himself of no reputation, and took upon him the form of a servant, and was made in the likeness of men."
(Philippians 2:5-7 KJV)

"For who hath known the mind of the Lord, that he may instruct him? but we have the mind of Christ."
(1 Corinthians 2:16 KJV)

The love we hold for God is fully realized through His Word, because the Father, the Word, and the Holy Spirit are one (1 John 5:7). We present ourselves as a living sacrifice holy and acceptable to Him. We are no longer conformed to this world, but we are changed by renewing our minds with His Word so that we are able to prove what is the good, acceptable, and perfect will of God. Please take note that God has no "permissive" will as I have heard spoken so many times. By His own Writings — the Bible — His will is good, acceptable, and perfect. Oh, certainly, we have been given the will to choose: *"I call heaven and earth to record this day against you, that I have set before you life and death, blessing and cursing: therefore choose life, that both thou and thy seed may live,"* (Deuteronomy 30:19 KJV).

God has given us this free will. Then, He goes on to suggest that we choose life . . . He simply tells us what He recommends. God will not interfere with the choice you make. However, if you make the wrong choice, you will suffer the consequences. This, my friend, is not God "permitting" you to make the wrong choice, so there is no "permissive will". This is YOUR CHOICE when making the wrong decision, because you did not follow God's instructions, e.g., His Word. Therefore, you were operating in the realm of disobedience. I reiterate, God's will is always good, acceptable, and perfect!

Since we have endeavored to allow the love of God to radiate through our lives because we love Him with all our hearts and all our souls, our minds now dictate to our entire being what and how it is to think, and what it will receive or reject. We now bless the Lord with all our souls and everything that is within us, and every organ in our body leaps to the safety line of divine health.

> *"Bless the LORD, O my soul: and all that is within me, bless his holy name. Bless the LORD, O my soul, and forget not all his benefits: Who forgiveth all thine iniquities; who healeth all thy diseases."*
> (Psalm 103:1-3 KJV)

Surely, He heals all of our diseases.

Once you allow your spirit to take on the nature of God, you begin to walk in His Spirit. Flesh has no more control over your life, and you enjoy the fruit of the spirit, which is love, joy, peace, longsuffering, gentleness, goodness, faith, meekness, and temperance (Galatians 5:22-23). Such glorious activity in the brain influences the body to release chemicals which intensify the bone marrow, causing it to manufacture healthy bone cells, bringing about a high level of functioning to our immune system. Also, by this we are able to see how our good thoughts work to produce divine health in our bodies.

Chapter Six

CHILDLIKE FAITH

"Except ye be converted, and become as little children, ye shall not enter into the kingdom of heaven. Whosoever therefore shall humble himself as this little child, the same is greatest in the kingdom of heaven."
(Matthew 18:3-4 KJV)

The gentleness of God is so dear that it melts your heart. If we could only understand that all God asks of us is to remain innocent, pure, humble, and trusting. Many of us want to be super giants in the Kingdom, but the truth is, the more childlike we become, the more God can use us. Jesus made it so plain when He explained to His disciples, *". . . Except ye be converted, and become as little children, ye shall not enter into the kingdom of heaven. Whosoever therefore shall humble himself as this little child, the same is greatest in the kingdom of heaven."* (Matthew 18:3-4 KJV)

Years ago, I was just growing in my Christian walk and had read through the Bible at least once. I had no real training as to how to cooperate with the Holy Spirit, but one thing I did have was trust. I had placed my life in God's hands, and my childlike faith believed that it would receive anything it asked of a loving Father. I recall exercising in the guest bedroom one afternoon, and while riding the stationery bike, I noticed that varicose veins had threaded their way up and down both of my thighs. I stopped riding the bike, placed my hands on both thighs, and looked up to the heavens. *Father, I will do what I can do and lose this weight;*

You take these varicose veins away for me. It was a very unemotional and simple request. With no afterthought, I went about my affairs during the next few days. The very next time I put on those shorts and began riding the bike, I naturally looked down at my thighs, and what do you know, no blue-green pipelines. Those limbs were as smooth and as clear as velvet. Just like that, I simply asked God to take the veins away, and He did. No fuss, no hassle, no waiting, not even a reflection, and zip, the veins had disappeared. Gently, tenderly, lovingly, they were washed away at the voice of one simple request. *"Ask, and it shall be given you; seek, and ye shall find; knock, and it shall be opened unto you,"* (Matthew 7:7 KJV). I believe that God granted me this request because my heart simply had a desire. It was not a vanity request to show off, but just something I wanted to make me feel better. As any good father would do, He honored my request because He wanted His child to feel better about herself.

God is not always so gentle, though. Jesus admonished Peter, *" . . . Simon, Simon, behold, Satan hath desired to have you, that he may sift you as wheat: But I have prayed for thee, that thy faith fail not: and when thou art converted, strengthen thy brethren,"* (Luke 22:31-32 KJV). Notice, Jesus did not address Peter by the name Peter, which is translated little rock, or Cephas, the Aramaic version of Peter, but He called him Simon. Not only did He call Peter Simon, but he also called the name out twice — an indication of urgency. Whether audibly or in your spirit, if you've ever heard God warn you, then you know that He doesn't speak gently at all.

It is outside the realm of healing, but I would like to share with you an example of one of my own personal experiences of how abrasive God can be. God had clearly instructed me to write *Mr$. Rafton, Sowing and Reaping,* an exposé of corruption among professionals in long-term care facilities, based upon my many years of experience as a nursing home administrator. Prior to self publishing the book, I had written to at least 150 agents and publishers, only to be rejected. I got so angry with God for not publishing the book that one night, out of desperation, I literally screamed at Him, *Lord, You told me to write this book. Now when are You going to publish it?!* Far louder and with a thunderous rippling roar, the Holy Spirit retorted with a few simple, but oh, so piercing words: "Wait for me to instruct; I will surely let you know!" God always confirms His Word:

> *"I will instruct you and teach you in the way you should go; I will guide you with My eye."*
> (Psalm 32:8 NKJV)

> *"The LORD thundered from heaven, and the most High uttered his voice. And he sent out arrows, and scattered them; lightning, and discomfited them."*
> (2 Samuel 22:14-15 KJV)

The words were spoken by Him with anger and resentment, as if to say, *"How dare you not trust Me!"* Both frightened and shocked, I fell to my knees in tears and embarrassment, repenting all the while. I heard what God was saying and understood the seriousness of being patient.

The name Simon means "to hear" [1], and for Jesus to have spoken the name twice in succession signifies that He wanted to put a halt to Peter's impetuosity and receive his undivided attention: "Simon, Simon," i.e., *Listen, listen, and hear every word I am speaking to you! satan wants to grind you to smithereens and blast you away, but I have prayed that you stand in unwavering faith on the Words you have learned from Me.* All the while, Jesus knew that He had gotten Peter's undivided attention because He did not say 'if' you are converted . . ." but rather, 'when' you are converted . . . ."

The key is, we must bear the name of "Simon" and have an ear to hear. Once we hear with revelatory ears or our spirit ears, we will respond as Peter responded and follow God's commands.

When God instructs us to live a life of faith, He doesn't mean that we should operate in faith in a few selected areas of our life and omit the others. He means that we should operate in faith in our health as well as in our wealth. Just as He promises that riches and honor are in our house in Psalm 112, He also promises in Psalm 107:20 that He has sent His Word and healed us and delivered us from our destruction. The Gospel is good news, and it is an all-encompassing full Gospel brought to us to set the captives free in all areas of life. The prophet Isaiah foretold that Jesus would come to give us full liberty:

> *"The Spirit of the Lord God is upon me, because the Lord has anointed and qualified me to preach the Gospel of good tidings to the meek, the poor, and afflicted; He has sent me to bind up and heal the brokenhearted, to proclaim liberty to the [physical and spiritual] captives and the opening of the prison and of the eyes to those who are bound, To proclaim the acceptable year of the Lord [the year of His favor] and the day of vengeance of our God, to comfort all who mourn, To grant [consolation and joy] to those who mourn in Zion--to give them an ornament (a garland or diadem) of beauty instead of ashes, the oil of joy instead of mourning, the garment [expressive] of praise instead of a heavy, burdened, and failing spirit--that they may be called oaks of righteousness [lofty, strong, and magnificent, distinguished for uprightness, justice, and right standing with God], the planting of the Lord, that He may be glorified."*
>
> (Isaiah 61:1-3 AMP)

This prophesy was confirmed in Luke 4:18-21, where it is written that Jesus had just completed 40 days of fasting and prayer while in the wilderness and came out to begin His earthy ministry. His bold and confident announcement told the world that no sickness, doubt, oppression, subjugation, fear, insecurity, poverty, or any other damaging thing could succeed in the Kingdom of God. *"For all the promises of God in Him are Yes, and in Him Amen, to the glory of God through us,"* (2 Corinthians 1:20 NKJV). As we live a life of faith in Christ Jesus, it gives the Father great pleasure to bless us so that we can glorify Him.

You have probably heard someone say that God gave them a sickness or a disease so He could get their attention or so they would slow down and listen to Him — or some other self-serving explanation. Why on Earth would a great and wonderful God take the devil's destructive tools and force injury, damage, sickness, or even death on one of His children in order to get their attention? Do you think that God who is brilliant enough to create the worlds and everything in them doesn't have intelligence enough to call your name and get your attention? Would you take a pit bull's teeth and plunge them into the neck of your little one so that you can get your child's attention? Would you take your 3-year-old son and plunge him into the Atlantic Ocean in mid-January in temperatures below freezing with no clothes on and no life jacket in order to get his attention? That's a sure invitation to death, and that's exactly what the thief comes to do: steal, kill, and destroy (John 10:10). You would never dream of subjecting your child to harm! Then what makes you think that a righteous and holy and loving God would cause you such pains or dangers? Selah!

God doesn't use satan's instruments to force you to love Him or spend time with Him, does He? No! All you do for God is done by choice. Prior to marriage, you wouldn't want to place a gun in your future spouse's head and demand that he or she marry you, would you?

God has never failed and He never will, period. The truth of the matter is, God can't fail because God is a sovereign, self-governing God, subject only to Himself or submitting only to Himself. In other words, God responds according to what is in

Him and according to that part of Himself which He has revealed to us. In brief, God responds to His Word. Jesus, having been sent to Earth to represent God, solidly embraced His role as God the man, and not once did He consider doing anything separate and aside from God, His Father.

> *"Then Jesus answered and said to them, 'Most assuredly, I say to you, the Son can do nothing of Himself, but what He sees the Father do; for whatever He does, the Son also does in like manner.' "*
>
> (John 5:19 NKJV)

Jesus has left the third part of the triune God to reside in us in the person of the Holy Spirit, the One who teaches us all things. We should never make a move unless we have consulted Him.

> *"But the Helper, the Holy Spirit, whom the Father will send in My name, He will teach you all things, and bring to your remembrance all things that I said to you."*
>
> (John 14:26 NKJV)

Jesus only responds to the Father, and He has given us countless examples in His Word encouraging us to do likewise.

In all essence, submitting yourself to God is a delight, once you understand your relationship to Him and how you are positioned in Him. Offering yourself to Him as a living sacrifice is now second nature, because God becomes your life, and the life you live is automatically lived by faith through Christ Jesus. This is why the Apostle Paul writes that we can do all things through Christ Jesus who strengthens us. When you acknowledge, without exception, that you have been purchased with a price, you no longer belong to yourself; it becomes an unequivocal honor to yield your members to God, the person to whom they belong.

When we submit ourselves to God, we invoke His divine protection, closing the door to all of satan's entries into our affairs, and that includes our health. Submitting to God causes the Word of God to be lifted from the pages of the Bible, to be converted from the metamorphosis of sheer doctrinal rhetoric turning into a river of life springing up in us, and emitting blasts of dynamite, or dunamis powers, from our mouths into any ungodly situation. Acts 1:8 says that we shall receive power after the Holy Ghost has come upon us, and that power in the Greek is dunamis, which means dynamite. I have never known dynamite not to be explosive, have you? It is time that we begin to look inside ourselves and evaluate the one who is residing within us — and what it is that He has equipped us with. Submitting to God causes Him to perfect everything concerning us, as He promises: *"The Lord will perfect that which concerns me: thy mercy O Lord, endures forever: forsake not the works of thine own hands,"* (Psalm 138:8 KJV). His hands in motion causes the universe to rotate on its axis, so you can just imagine how effortless it is for Him to stabilize all situations in our lives, including the reformation of cells in our bodies. When we are in a true place of submission, we understand that satan has no place in us, and we choose to live a life pleasing to God so that God can bring constant renewal and promotion into our lives for His glory.

Submitting to God especially means that we consistently practice a life of love. Our daily walk must emulate Christ's love in such a manner that people will know we are not of this world. We must love with an irresistible commitment to please God.

> *"By this shall all men know that ye are my disciples, if ye have love one to another."*
> (John 13:35 KJV)

> *"He that hath my commandments, and keepeth them, he it is that loveth me: and he that loveth me shall be loved of my Father; and I will love him, and will manifest myself to him. . . . If a man love me, he will keep my words . . ."*
> (John 14:21,23 KJV)

Loving God first is simply obeying Him or doing just what it is He tells you to do.

"If you love Me, you will keep my commandments."

(John 14:15)

Because of the lifestyle we have chosen to live, satan must back up the minute we apply God's Word to our situation, or even sooner. Our Christian walk automatically repels satan's attacks through our confession, because with the mouth, confession is made unto salvation (deliverance), as promised in Romans 10:10. Therefore, we should outright refuse to accept satan's attack(s), and when we let him know that we refuse to accept his attack(s), he VANISHES!

"Submit yourselves therefore to God. Resist the devil, and he will flee from you."

(James 4:7 KJV)

Chapter Seven

HOODWINKED

"Nevertheless they did flatter him with their mouth, and
they lied unto him with their tongues."

(Psalm 78:36 KJV)

W hat sort of medication costs ten thousand dollars for a single month's supply? Thirty tiny pills for $10,000 is what I'm talking about, folks. This was the price quoted to me by a customer who recently visited our health food store. It may be that there are some in the medicine manufacturing or distribution field who are able to produce names of drugs that are worth that much, but I certainly have strong reservations about that. Such a price tag for a thirty-day supply of medication (or any other single consumable product, for that matter) is so excessive that it reaches beyond inflation and plunges into corrupt misrepresentation, more commonly labeled as fraud.

In fact, just recently, I was watching CNN when one of the guests mentioned that AARP was investigating a charge for a cancer medication in excess of $200 and vying for a reduction in cost. This contemplated action, by the mere fact of its mention, confirms my theory of the appalling price tag affixed to the customer's ten grand monthly medication. If a person took the time to research the ingredients going into the manufacturing process of medications, I can almost assure you that there would be no pill worth a $10,000 monthly charge, or $333.33 per pill, to be exact.

As He does to me, I pray that the Holy Spirit will nudge the people who are reading this book to pray that God will continue exposing all corruption in the medical industry. God promises that we can be sure our sins are exposed: " . . . *ye have sinned against the Lord: and be sure your sin will find you out,*" (Numbers 32:23 KJV). He also promises: *"For there is nothing hid, which shall not be manifested; neither was anything kept secret, but that it should come abroad,"* (Mark 4:22 KJV) (See also Luke 8:17).

> *". . . if my people, who are called by my name, will humble themselves and pray and seek my face and turn from their wicked ways, then will I hear from heaven and will forgive their sin and will heal their land."*
> (2 Chronicles 7:14 NIV)

Based on this verse, God wants His people to pray against all unrighteousness, whether it is adultery, mislabeling of foods, substance abuse, pushing cocaine, contributing toward any form of drug or substance abuse, Medicare fraud, deceit within the Internal Revenue Service, or illegal and sinful medical practices. Just as God wants illegal drugs removed from the streets, He also wants medical doctors to practice with honesty and integrity. Overpricing medications is a sin in the Eyes of God, and so is prescribing medications that will bring harm to the patient's body. When we as ambassadors of Christ realize what the problems are, it is our responsibility to pray that God will put an end to such practices. We cannot afford to discuss the problem as a measure of criticism or merely complain for the sake of complaining. When we do, we are feeding into the hands of the Devil.

> *"Come near, ye nations, to hear; and hearken, ye people: let the earth hear, and all that is therein; the world, and all things that come forth of it."*
> (Isaiah 34:1 KJV)

The Earth has ears, and it listens to all that is introduced throughout its atmosphere. When we complain or gossip, we perpetuate the problem, and it spreads throughout the Earth. As Christians and ambassadors for Christ, we are sent here to rule over the Earth and stop the problems, not perpetuate them. Our responsibility is to bind everything that misrepresents God and pray that He will heal the problems. When we complain, the wind of our breath carries the problem throughout the Earth and compounds the damage already brewing. The Earth doesn't have a mind to discern what is good or what is evil; it only has ears to carry forth what it has heard.

Matured saints of God do not carry messages that go against God's Word; instead, they take authority over the problem. When we fully understand what God meant when He said He "calls things that are not as though they were" (Romans 4:17 NIV), we will see the world around us in a vast array of grandeur. It is truly time for the saints of God to cause Heaven to manifest itself here on Earth, and this will be accomplished through our prayers and conversation.

> "... because the creation itself also will be delivered from the bondage of corruption into the glorious liberty of the children of God. For we know that the whole creation groans and labors with birth pangs together until now. Not only that, but we also who have the firstfruits of the Spirit, even we ourselves groan within ourselves, eagerly waiting for the adoption, the redemption of our body."
> (Romans 8:21-23 NKJV)

Not only does the Earth have ears, but also as an element of creation; it is groaning and travailing, pressing and pushing through the conflicts within the atmosphere, waiting for us to bring Heaven down to Earth.

War in Washington

Around the time I was first introduced to nutritional supplements, certain senators began fighting to protect the medical industry. They fought to pass laws that would force our citizens to get a prescription for vitamins and herbs, which are food supplements. You must understand that health food stores are licensed by the Department of Agriculture, the same industry that licenses grocery stores.

The omnipotent, all-knowing God never ceases to amaze me. From the portals of Heaven, at the beginning of Creation, He looked down into the 21st century and saw the deceptive minds of men. He knew exactly what would happen, and long before the alternative healing practices resurfaced (I say 're-surfaced' because herbs were God's initial plan to allow the human race to walk in divine health.), God laid in Zion a cornerstone for anyone attempting to block the natural health of His people. God saw to it that man could not patent the foods that grew on His good Earth. Unfortunately, as recently as February of 2010, Senator John McCain introduced another bill to infringe upon the health of Americans and to protect the medical industry. In a report by OnlinePRNews.com, the author writes:

> *Senator McCain Files New Bill That Attacks Your Access to Supplements. Bill Would Repeal Key Sections of the Dietary Supplement Health and Education Act.*
>
> *Online PR News – 05-February-2010* – Washington, DC: Senator John McCain has introduced a bill called The Dietary Supplement Safety Act (DSSA). DSSA would repeal key sections of the Dietary Supplement Health and Education Act (DSHEA) and significantly diminish access to a broad range of dietary supplements, according to the Alliance for Natural Health USA. (ANH-USA)

"If passed as written, this bill would likely
result in the disappearance from store shelves of
many supplements currently on the market, and
unbridled authority would be handed to the FDA,
an agency that needs a top to bottom overhaul, not
ever more power over our lives," added Gretchen
DuBeau, executive director for ANH-USA.

It seems that some of our elected officials are more interested
in financially supporting the personal needs of giant gougers over
the health and welfare of the very American people who put them
in office. Clearly, official representatives such as Senator McCain
are attempting to find ways to regulate the health supplement
industry more and more. Did our lawmakers not read that you
cannot curse what God has blessed?

After being flooded with tens of thousands of e-mails
protesting his attack on the nutritional supplement industry,
Senator McCain finally backed out of supporting a bill which
he had personally introduced to the lawmakers. Thank God
for organizations such as the Alliance for Natural Health-USA
who eyed this slippery bill, which would have given the FDA
enormous control over the natural health industry.

Not only was this bill quashed, but more recently the federal
courts found that the FDA's complaints against vitamin health
claims were unconstitutional:

ANH-USA Wins Major Lawsuit on Qualified Health Claims

April 19, 2011

We took 'em to court—and we won! A federal court
has found the FDA's stance against vitamin health
claims to be unconstitutional!

On April 13, the United States District Court for the District of Columbia held that the FDA's denial of two health claims—which dealt with the ability of antioxidant vitamins to reduce the risk of cancer—was unconstitutional under the First Amendment.

ANH-USA, together with Durk Pearson and Sandy Shaw, sued the FDA for censoring antioxidant vitamin–cancer risk reduction claims after the agency denied multiple claims about the effectiveness of selenium and vitamins C and E in reducing cancer risk, and weakened and complicated other claims to the vanishing point. The plaintiffs were represented by Emord & Associates, a prominent constitutional law firm. You may recall that last October on the selenium claim. That win means that selenium supplements are now allowed to claim that "selenium may reduce the risk" of prostate, colon, bladder, or thyroid cancer.

"Qualified health claims" characterize the relationship between a substance and its ability to reduce the risk of a disease or health-related condition. They are permitted in relation to foods and supplements—a precedent established by the landmark decision of Pearson v. Shalala. Qualified health claims are a critical means toward communicating important health benefits of natural foods and dietary supplements otherwise forbidden by the FDA. Unfortunately, the FDA has consistently limited the information available to consumers about the real health benefits of food and supplements and routinely rejects all qualified health claims. This should come as no surprise, given that the FDA has worked shoulder-to-shoulder with the European Commission for well over a decade agreeing on ridiculously onerous guidelines for scientific substantiation of health claims internationally in the Codex Alimentarius. These requirements have been carbon-copied into EU law and sometime next year will ban thousands of claims that have informed European citizens for years. We must stop trans-Atlantic European regulatory creep at all costs, and our biggest defense remains our precious First Amendment.

Although the District Court for the District of Columbia upheld FDA censorship of six other claims, the court ruled that the FDA violated the First Amendment when it prohibited two vitamin health claims and stated that it would allow them in a form reworded by the agency:

Vitamin C / gastric cancer claim: "Vitamin C may reduce the risk of gastric cancer."

• FDA had prohibited the claim, stating that it would only allow the following language to be used: "One weak study and one study with inconsistent results suggest that vitamin C supplements may reduce the risk of gastric cancer. Based on these studies, FDA concludes that it is highly uncertain that vitamin C supplements reduce the risk of gastric cancer."

Vitamin E / bladder cancer claim: "Vitamin E may reduce the risk of bladder cancer."

• FDA had prohibited the claim, stating that it would only allow the following language to be used: "One small study suggests that vitamin E supplements may reduce the risk of bladder cancer. However, two small studies showed no reduction of risk. Based on these studies, FDA concludes that it is highly unlikely that vitamin E supplements reduce the risk of bladder cancer."

The court held FDA's rewording of the two claims unconstitutional under the First Amendment. FDA "has replaced plaintiffs' claims entirely," explained the court, and the qualifying the claim so completely "effectively negates any relationship between cancer risk and vitamin intake. The FDA's rewording . . . makes it difficult to tell what the original health claims are and appears to disavow the FDA's own conclusions that those claims are supported by credible evidence."

The court reaffirmed Pearson v. Shalala against the FDA's objections, holding that "where the evidence supporting a claim is inconclusive, the First Amendment permits the claim to be made; the FDA cannot require a disclaimer that simply swallows the claim." The FDA has been ordered to revise its claim qualifications consistent with the court's decision . . .

(http://www.anh-usa.org/anh-usa-wins-major-lawsuit-on-qualified-health-claims/)

The spirit that caused the Philistines to make war against themselves is now spreading through the hearts of some of our government leaders: First, Senator McCain introduces a law against the health industry but then turns around and repeals his very own law. Next, the FDA files a legal claim that vitamin C, selenium, and vitamin E have no health benefits for fighting cancer but later disavows its very own conclusions because it had to admit to credible evidence of the effectiveness of these nutrients. Why would the agency, formed to protect the health of its nation, fight against what is best for its people? Why would such an agency make all-out attempts to hide the truth about health benefits? When we view such actions from a spiritual perspective, we see that this is as demonic as they come. To know

God's position in a matter and continue to war against what is right is another way of mocking Him:

> *"But, beloved, remember ye the words which were spoken before of the apostles of our Lord Jesus Christ; How that they told you there should be mockers in the last time, who should walk after their own ungodly lusts."*
>
> (Jude 1:17-18 KJV)

One day at the shop, I was talking to Troy Reynolds, a friend of mine, about corruption within the health regulatory industry. Troy made the most profound statement: "The government is regulating deadly foods such as sugar and so on and forcing us to subsidize the cost."

My mind immediately drifted to meats with steroids and genetically modified vegetables and fruits. A genetically modified organism (GMO), as defined by Wikipedia, is:

". . . an organism whose genetic material has been altered using genetic engineering techniques. These techniques, generally known as recombinant DNA technology, use DNA molecules from different sources, which are combined into one molecule to create a new set of genes. This DNA is then transferred into an organism, giving it modified or novel genes. Transgenic organisms, a subset of GMOs, are organisms that have inserted DNA from a different species. GMOs are the constituents of genetically modified foods."

Chief demon satan comes as an angel of light under the guise of law, life, and healing, but he brings with him injustice, death, and sickness. Whatever goes against God's Word only produces death, no matter how it's packaged.

WHATEVER GOES AGAINST GOD'S WORD PRODUCES DEATH, NO MATTER HOW IT IS PACKAGED.

I cannot overemphasize the importance of our praying that God will continue to reveal every single sin in the medical industry as well as in the body of our government, including the FDA. We should pray against political conspiracy and that God will give us leaders who are pure, honest, and upright before Him. When the saints of God understand that no power is greater than the power of prayer, we will absolutely refuse to concur with the world's opinions; instead, we will get on our knees to pull down every existing wall of Jericho. We will refuse to continue giving our power to the enemy by repeating what we hear over the news, and we will work in the spirit realm to see that the captives are set free.

Research for Diseases — Is It A Trick?

Fortunately, there are industry workers helping to educate members of Congress and their staff about the natural health industry and its legislative priorities. Those in the health industry focus primarily on healthy lifestyles, raw foods, exercise, and dietary supplements as effective and preventive measures against diseases.

Long have I maintained that 'research organizations' in their claims to find 'cures' for diseases are actually fostering sicknesses instead of accepting proven cures. Take diabetes for example; thousands have reported having been healed by simply changing their diets, adding cinnamon and other nutrients to their daily intake, and by exercising. In fact, not a week passes that a customer does not come into our store to give a wonderful report that he or she has changed lifestyles and discontinued taking medications for diabetes. In Dr. Malkmus's books, *God's Way to Ultimate Health* and *Hallelujah Diet*, there are many testimonials from sufferers going off their medications and simply eating God's Way and exercising. Why don't diabetic research organizations report these types of healings, instead of endorsing medications which

LOLA HARDAWAY

they know for a fact are harmful? It is a proven fact that most medications for diabetes cause renal failure.

> *"And Jesus went with him; and much people followed him, and thronged him. And a certain woman, which had an issue of blood twelve years, And had suffered many things of many physicians, and had spent all that she had, and was nothing bettered, but rather grew worse."*
> (Mark 5:24-26 KJV)

How can a 'fight against cancer' warrant honor when it ignores evidence of sure cures? Nineteen years ago, Dr. Lorraine Day was diagnosed with terminal cancer and given a very short time to live. She is an internationally acclaimed orthopedic trauma surgeon who was on the faculty of the UCSF School of Medicine, Chief of Orthopedic Surgery at San Francisco General Hospital, and Vice Chairman of the Department of Orthopedics. With these impressive credentials, it is certain that she consulted the best physicians in the industry. Yet, just as the woman with the issue of blood sought many physicians and did not get better, so did Dr. Day consult with the best only to receive a death notice.

It is wonderful that Dr. Day is a Bible-believing Christian. I recall reading that she immersed herself in the Holy Bible, meditating specifically on God's healing promises, day in and day out. In addition, she completely changed her diet to 70% raw fruits and vegetables, along with plenty of quality water. The cooked foods she consumed were those grown in the ground and not from animals. Needless to say, she consumed no sugar whatsoever; sugar is to cancer as kerosene is to fire. It was just that simple.

> *"When she had heard of Jesus, came in the press behind, and touched his garment. For she said, If I may touch but his clothes, I shall be whole. And straightway the fountain of her blood was dried up; and she felt in her body that she was healed of that plague."*
> (Mark 5:27-29 KJV)

120

As it relates to God's Word, what did she do? Dr. Day touched the hem of Jesus' garment and was made whole, just as was the woman with the issue of blood. Touching the hem of Jesus' garment merely means that you are putting Him in remembrance of His Promises, standing on His Word without wavering. It means that you are certain that what He has promised in His Word will transfer into your life because the Word is life, and as you speak God's Word, you are pouring life into your body! (See also John 6:63.)

Dr. Lorraine Day's remedy for cancer was simply God's prescription for healing:

> "Fruit trees of all kinds will grow on both banks of the river. Their leaves will not wither, nor will their fruit fail. Every month they will bear, because the water from the sanctuary flows to them. **Their fruit will serve for food and their leaves for healing.**"
>
> (Ezekiel 47:12 NIV, bold mine)

'Organizations' do not conduct research, but doctors and scientists do. If these organizations pointed to the real truth in healing, I believe health would reach a new plateau in our society. If they continue to turn their backs on love, truth, and hope for our people, the abyss is inevitable for such groups. As our Congress continues to apply God's dietary laws to its health and nutrition plan, we will realize a savings of billions of dollars in medical expense.

> "He causes the grass to grow for the cattle, And vegetation for the service of man, That he may bring forth food from the earth."
>
> (Psalm 104:14 NKJV)

The research was already done prior to the Creation of man. Oh, that we would only rejoice in and enjoy the simple but miraculous life which God has already provided!

"O that men would praise [and confess to] the Lord for His goodness and loving-kindness and His wonderful works to the children of men! For He satisfies the longing soul and fills the hungry soul with good.

. . . He saved them out of their distress. He brought them out of darkness and the shadow of death and broke apart the bonds that held them.

He sends forth His word and heals them and rescues them from the pit and destruction. Oh that men would praise [and confess to] the Lord for His goodness and loving kindness and His wonderful works to the children of men!

He turns a wilderness into a pool of water and a dry ground into water springs. And there He makes the hungry to dwell, that they may prepare a city for habitation, And sow fields, and plant vineyards which yield fruits of increase. He blesses them also so that they are multiplied greatly, and allows not their cattle to decrease.

. . . He raises the poor and needy from affliction and makes their families like a flock. The upright shall see it and be glad, but all iniquity shall shut its mouth. Whoso is wise [if there be any truly wise] will observe and heed these things, and they will diligently consider the mercy and loving-kindness of the Lord."

(Psalm 107:8-9,13-14,20-21,35-38,41-43 AMP)

Conventional Medicine Can't Heal Anyone of Anything

I cannot tell you how often I have heard someone say, "My blood pressure is perfect." I usually examine their exterior and ask, "Are you taking medications from the doctor for your blood pressure?" I'm almost always right; the only person who answered 'no' later confessed to her pastor that she had not told the truth. When you have worked in the industry as long as I have, it is not difficult to look at a person's countenance and know whether or not they are taking conventional medications.

Under no circumstance is your blood pressure 'normal' or 'perfect' if you are taking high blood pressure medications to control it. In fact, you are a prime candidate for congestive heart failure. I have not found a single beta blocker or high blood pressure medication that will not cause such side effects as fluid build-up, swelling throughout the body, especially around the heart and ankles, renal failure, Alzheimer's disease, and/or many other serious problems.

I could not resist including an article I recently downloaded from my e-mail, written by Dr. George Malkmus of Hallelujah Acres. Again I say, if you have not already purchased Dr. Malkmus's book, *The Hallelujah Diet,* I strongly recommend that you do, because there is no better information available for natural healing, and I cannot think of a better place for you to start learning about healing your body:

Conventional Medicine Can't Heal Anyone of Anything OR Living In An Age of Contradiction

The following is an excerpt from *101 Great Ways to Improve Your Health* by David Riklan and Dr. Joseph Cilea:

"We live in an age of contradiction. Never has such a wonderfully diverse wealth of information about health been so easily accessible. Never have we known more of the secrets of the human body. And yet, never have so many Americans been making so many bad decisions about their health.

Today, according to the National Center for Health Statistics, about two-thirds of U.S. adults are overweight or obese - 133.6 million people in all.

A new study completed by the National cancer Institute indicates that 40.93% of men and women born today will be diagnosed with cancer at some time during their lifetime.

Someone dies of heart disease every 34 seconds.

One in six Americans is either pre-diabetic or diabetic.

Over ten million Americans are taking anti-depressants.

One in six Americans suffer from an anxiety disorder.

And incidence rates of conditions like childhood diabetes, sleep disorders, Alzheimer's, anxiety and depression are spiraling upward with shocking speed.

Why are so many of us so unhealthy? . . . Health awareness is the first step in the [right] path.

Hallelujah Acres' mission is to empower you with **information that will enable you to make informed and biblically sound choices**.

If the mounting tide of disease is to be stopped, **each individual must take responsibility for their health** and make informed choices that will enable the innate, self-healing God placed within each body to function as designed.

When this takes place, we can not only avoid the ravages of those diseases but **most often reverse the disease state** that is manifesting symptoms.

Never have we known more of the secrets of the human body. And yet, never have so many Americans been making so many bad decisions about their health. "

www.hacres.com

As Dr. Malkmus points out, there is so much information available to us today, yet we choose to ignore it.

> *"There will be a highway called the Holy Road. No one rude or rebellious is permitted on this road. It's for God's people exclusively— impossible to get lost on this road. Not even fools can get lost on it."*
> (Isaiah 35:8 MSG)

God has made the way so plain; the simple reality of most sicknesses goes back to God's Word:

> *"My people are destroyed for lack of knowledge; because you [the priestly nation] have rejected knowledge, I will also reject you that you shall be no priest to Me; seeing you have forgotten the law of your God, I will also forget your children."*
> (Hosea 4:6 AMP)

In the very beginning, when He had Moses to write the Book of Genesis, God issued dietary laws. Granted, faith comes by hearing, and one must hear and hear and hear, over and over again, before faith in what he or she hears becomes evident. On a personal note, it generally takes two or three times for me to hear new information before it registers, but after that, I get it.

In today's world, nutritional healing, often referred to as 'alternative' or 'holistic' healing, is no longer debatable. Sickness is sin, and when one rejects God's healing plan, which He so clearly laid out in Genesis, his or her thoughts are being controlled by the devil.

"[s]atan, who is the god of this world, has blinded the minds of those who don't believe. They are unable to see the glorious light of the Good News. They don't understand this message about the glory of Christ, who is the exact likeness of God."

(2 Corinthians 4:4 NLT)

When the Apostle writes that *". . . they don't understand this message about the glory of Christ,"* Paul is referring to the countless benefits available to us through His Blood, which Christ Jesus shed at Calvary. The thirty-nine stripes Jesus bore on His body included every sickness mentionable; yet many Christians do not understand — or even want to understand — the significance of the precious Blood Jesus shed for our sins, which includes sickness. Too many refuse to open their mouths and 'speak' the Gospel out loud, claiming God's Promises for their lives. A spirit of pride will trick them into believing that just thinking God's Word is just as effective as speaking it. No, it is not the same. Learn to obey God's dietary laws and watch the Glory of God change your life. Obedience to all of the Gospel is our sure key to victory.

Quality nutritional supplements — that's whole food vitamins, herbs, minerals, and proteins — have taken our world by storm and become part of the mainstream. This means that a huge number of people all over the world have chosen to take their lives into their own hands and are using quality nutrients for health maintenance. These people understand that quality nutritional supplements help to prevent diseases from forming in the body, help to aid in healing the body without causing side effects, help to make them feel good, and help to enhance their lifespan. Today, people are living longer, and this includes physicians. In fact, the National Census Bureau reports that the average lifespan has taken a quantum leap from fifty-seven years to seventy-four for men and seventy-nine for women.[2]

Thank God, also, that He is raising up holistic medical doctors in the universe, and they are practicing preventive medicine by using nutritional supplements for alternative healing! God will never allow satan to outdo Him.

> *". . . but where sin abounded, grace did much more abound."*
>
> (Romans 5:20 KJV)

Sickness is sin, and God has given us the prescription for health:

> *"In the midst of the street of it, and on either side of the river, was there the tree of life, which bare twelve manner of fruits, and yielded her fruit every month; and the leaves of the tree were for the healing of the nations."*
>
> (Revelation 22:2 KJV)

It is on Earth as it is in Heaven. God has given us the leaves for medicine. The simple fact is that unprocessed, uncooked green foods bring healing to the body.

Who Would Dare Challenge God?

> *"And by the river upon the bank thereof, on this side and on that side, shall grow all trees for meat, whose leaf shall not fade, neither shall the fruit thereof be consumed: it shall bring forth new fruit according to his months, because their waters they issued out of the sanctuary: and the fruit thereof shall be for meat, and the leaf thereof for medicine."*
>
> (Ezekiel 47:12 KJV)

Whose report will you believe? It seems that many so-called healings prescribed by those who are practicing conventional medicine are in direct conflict with God's Word. A few years ago, the medical industry rumored that vitamin E was damaging to the body. When the Alliance for Natural Health intervened and presented mounds of evidence that vitamin E actually helped to support the cardiovascular system, causing the blood to flow and convey flexibility in the walls of the arteries, rumors ceased. It was suggested that not enough people were suffering with strokes and other heart diseases, and that corrupt officials in the medical industry sought to instill a level of fear into the general public that would cause them to stop taking vitamin E. This demonic spear of deception almost took hold, but it was through much prayer and cooperation within the nutritional supplement industry that the lie was bunged.

I frequently wonder what goes through the minds of doctors and scientists when they promote short-term fixes over long-term healing by advising kidney patients not to drink water or *stay away from green foods*. According to God, it is the green foods that nourish and heal the body. So, who will you put your confidence in: God or the doctor?

Here's the deal: Some doctors and scientists are out to make a name for themselves. When a synthetic product is invented that shows promise in one area of the body, the negative side of that invention is more or less suppressed for the sake of recognition and fame. Temporary relief is by no means comparable to healing. I simply never understood why one would substitute healing nutrients for an artificial, synthetic patch-up. I firmly believe that every organ in the body will restore itself when the counterfeit is withdrawn and God's healing foods are fed to the body.

> *"Children, obey your parents in the Lord: for this is right."*
>
> (Ephesians 6:1 KJV)

What bothers me even more is the question, "Why would a child of God prefer any plan other than that which God has established for his or her life?" I believe that when God said, *"Children, obey your parents,"* He included Himself, since He is our Father and we are His children. Most of us know that this is God's Commandment, issued with a promise, and the promise is that you will live a long life.

There are no greater medicines than those that grow in God's good earth. We should be grateful to God for giving scientists the technology and expertise to preserve and bottle many herbs and vitamins for our consumption. It is important to note that taking good nutritional supplements should always be accompanied with healthy, nutritious foods — especially raw foods — and daily exercise.

Buyer Beware

I cannot address the subject of nutritional supplements without issuing a 'buyer beware' warning: There are far too many companies in the industry that label their vitamin supplements 'healthy' even though they are manufactured with inferior, synthetic ingredients, including plastic and asphalt. That's right! Some include tar, and it is physically impossible for your body to absorb these chemically-produced products.

My cousin once took an extremely popular, commercially-manufactured vitamin, probably the most advertised in the media. When going to the doctor for X-rays, the doctor told her that the lining of her stomach was loaded with undigested vitamins. He went on to describe her stool as "like tiny pebbles". She hadn't told him that she took a supplement, yet he was absolutely correct. Needless to say, she reverted back to the whole food, quality vitamins. When taking synthetic supplements, the results could eventually be as damaging as taking conventional medications. Though the problem may appear 'patched up', the end results may not only be damaging but ultimately life threatening.

One of the largest manufacturers of conventional medications is the same manufacturer who makes the commercially-manufactured vitamin my cousin was taking, which probably out-sells any other vitamin on the mass market. More doesn't necessarily mean better. I feel that the medical industry foresaw the success of the new trend in the natural health market, and since these manufacturers were among the leaders in the medical industry, they were determined to gain a financial edge.

I speculate that since there were billions of dollars accessible to them for advertising, they usurped the market, leading the general public to believe that the highly advertised vitamins — not only the regular ones, but specialized brands promising benefits for seniors, menopausal females, men with at-risk prostates, and so on — were the cream of the crop, so to speak. People believe what they hear. The world wants to find someone it can trust. I say, if nutrients are designed to keep you well or to heal you, why is it necessary to continue taking conventional medications after you've faithfully taken the nutrients for six to twelve months? Selah!

With whole food nutrients, you will be safe, provided you change your eating and exercise habits. With synthetics, there is no chance you will ever be healed. What types of nutrients are you purchasing? Where do you purchase your nutrients? As a rule, the mass market will not provide you with quality nutrients or valuable information regarding the nutrients. For the most part, these venues promote synthetic vitamins and nutrients, and in many cases the staff is unskilled in promoting natural health products and haven't a clue as to what harm the synthetic vitamins are causing the customers.

I recall a young man who wandered into my shop a while back, asking me about this highly advertised renegade vitamin and wanting to know what I thought of it. When I told him that I felt that in the long run it could do more harm than good because it was made of synthetics, he agreed; "Lady, you are absolutely right. I used to work for their lab, and they put all kinds of garbage in the pills."

Something to Hide?

When I went to the Internet to search for the ingredients list for this specific manufacturer's well-advertised vitamin, I got a bunch of industry jargon. It went something like, "Specially formulated with key nutrients to help meet the nutritional needs of women fifty and over. Contains antioxidants that help support your immune function." To a layman this information sounds exciting, but to a health care professional, it is not only evasively shallow but also intellectually insulting, giving us little, if any, information about system support.

NOW Foods is a company owned and operated by Christians; they promote integrity first. When I conduct research on the Internet on their Multi-Food Complex multivitamin, they specify that the product consists of 75% organic ingredients, is fermented with whole food, has allergen-free probiotics, is a vegetarian formula, and many more descriptive system benefits. The label goes on to list the individual ingredients and informs the user of the number of units of each nutrient included in the product. The details published by NOW Foods is praiseworthy. Of utmost importance is that the vitamin has a whole food source.

Pharmaceutical companies are not the only companies producing inferior nutrients. We have a wonderful customer who has shopped at our store for at least fifteen years. One of the products she purchases routinely is calcium-magnesium, made by a nutritional manufacturing company, not a pharmaceutical company. On a few occasions she mentioned that her bone density was below average. I suggested that she switch the calcium-magnesium from the company she preferred to a specially formulated calcium microcrystalline hydroxyapatite (MCHA). (I recommend Life's Wonder's 'Wonder Bones', a MCHA that also helps strengthen cartilage and support the cardiovascular system.). I was first made aware of MCHA when Dr. Julian Whitaker produced a television show featuring Dr. Felton, who spent forty years in a research laboratory examining nothing but calciums. Dr. Felton, to my knowledge, was the first to discover that MCHA was far superior to other calciums. More recently, research published by Waitaki Bio Sciences, www.waitakibio.com/research/natural-calcium reveals the following for unprocessed bone proteins where the naturally occurring proteins have not been destroyed by heat:

> "Specifically, whole bone MCHA, with the naturally occurring bone proteins present, taken as a daily nutritional supplement has shown the following positive effects:
>
> Reduced loss of bone mineral density in postmenopausal women when taken in conjunction with Raloxifene *(Pelayo et al, 2008)*.
>
> Increased vertebral bone mass in post menopausal women when used in conjunction with hormone replacement therapy (Estradiol) to a greater extent than either treatment alone *(Castelo Branco et al, 1999)*.
>
> Increased bone mineral density in postmenopausal women with either below normal bone mineral density or inadequate dietary calcium intake *(Fernandez-Parejo et al, 2007)*.
>
> Prevented bone loss in a group of post menopausal women who had refused hormone replacement therapy *(Castelo Branco, 1999)*

Dramatically reduced skeletal (back) pain in a group of patients developing osteoporosis *(Pines et al, 1984)*.

Slowed the progression of osteoporosis in patients receiving long term corticosteroid treatment *(Pines et al, 1984)*.

Restored lost bone mineral density in a group of women on corticosteroid therapy for primary biliary cirrhosis *(Epstein et al, 1982)*.

Improved bone healing in rabbits with experimentally induced bone defects *(Annefeld et al, 1986)*.

Comparison to other forms of calcium supplementation

Whole bone MCHA has been compared to both calcium carbonate and calcium gluconate in clinical trials.

Four trials have compared MCHA to calcium carbonate, and in all four of these studies MCHA has shown superior performance at improving loss of bone mineral density in post menopausal women *(Pelayo et al 2008, Castelo Branco 1999, Ruegsegger et al 1995, Annefeld et al 1985)*.

There have been two published trials comparing MCHA to calcium gluconate. One of these studies demonstrated that whole bone MCHA was better than the equivalent amount of calcium gluconate at promoting the absorption of radio labeled calcium in elderly osteoporotic patients *(Windsor et al, 1973)*. In the second study, whole bone MCHA was able to restore lost bone mineral in a group of corticosteroid treated patients. Patients treated with calcium gluconate had their bone loss halted, but not restored *(Epstein et al, 1982)."*

Dr. Felton and others found that MCHA more closely matches human bones than any other on the market.

Lottie refused to listen. Prior to shopping at our store, she had shopped at a store where they convinced her that she was getting the best. 'Best' is not determined by how much commission the sales rep makes or how much of a discount the company is giving the health food store, but by the lab analysis and results experienced by the customers. I explained to her that she was purchasing an inferior product, but Lottie still did not listen.

Nearly a year later, Lottie came into the store, picked up her usual calcium-magnesium from the shelf, and told me that her doctor informed her, "Don't be surprised if your bones break while you are standing." Still, Lottie purchased the inferior product with the illusion that it was helping her. One may ask, "Why is your store carrying a product that you know is inferior?" Under normal circumstances, we do not stock such products, but if a customer insists, we will supply it to them, but we do not recommend it when educating other customers.

Many of us have heard stories where an older man or woman fell and broke his or her hip. The fact is, these stories are almost always twisted. This is satan's way of causing one to think that an accident occurred and caused one to fall, and that during the fall, he or she broke that hip bone. This is another trick from the devil!

What happened is just the opposite. First, the hip bone breaks, and then the victim no longer has structural support and a fall is inevitable. If bones become porous or brittle, with a sponge-like appearance, it means that they are weak and depleted of the proper calcium, phosphorus, and other minerals. Oftentimes, the individual has developed osteoporosis. When the condition exists over a prolonged period, the hip breaks. The solution is so simple; this can all be prevented by taking a good MCHA calcium.

Back to Lottie. Her condition was worsening, and this particular month she did not come into the store for her usual monthly purchase. She sent her daughter, instead, for her usual purchase, and if you know anything about older people, you dare not change the order. However, because Lottie had been such a faithful customer, I gifted her a bottle of MCHA with her regular order. Thank God — she took it. The next month, Lottie returned to the store, and this time she purchased the MCHA. Within one month, Lottie reported that the doctor said that her bones had hardened and were nearly normal!

Life's Wonder has a superior MCHA bone calcium called 'Wonder Bones', which is formulated with calcium-rich, high-collagen MCHA, the actual form of calcium found naturally in bone tissue. It provides both the organic and inorganic constituents found in one's skeletal structure. It also contains vitamin D_3 and trace minerals to help support calcium utilization. In addition to supporting the skeletal system, these other major minerals are a giant plus for cardiovascular support.

> *"For the love of money is a root of all kinds of evil, for which some have strayed from the faith in their greediness, and pierced themselves through with many sorrows."*
> (1 Timothy 6:10 NKJV)

It seems that some nutritional manufacturing companies are sacrificing quality for greed, and the bottom line is, they are really sacrificing their reputation. When saints such as you and I pray that God will expose all secret sin and heal the land, He often moves inside situations we could never imagine. This is why He urges us to pray in the Spirit so that the Holy Ghost is able to move wide and dig deep into the very core of the most remote and sophisticated operations, no matter what entity it might be.

Not only are there manufacturing companies producing inferior nutrients, but also many novice fortune-seekers today are jumping on the bandwagon at any cost. A few months back, a customer came into the store and asked for magnesium sulfate. This threw me for a loop. The conversation went something like this:

"You mean magnesium citrate?"

"No, sulfate."

"Oxide?"

"No, magnesium sulfate, and I want the powdered."

"I can't recall our using magnesium sulfate. Citrate, oxide, chloride, but not sulfate."

She was insistent. "They just advertised it on TV. They said you couldn't get it from the health food store; you had to order it from them. But, I know that if they have it, you have it. It has to be powder."

I showed her the powdered magnesium we had on the shelf, but it was not what she had been introduced to over the television. "Let me call the lab," I told her. "I'll get clarity on this." I telephoned the lab, and the nutritionist there laughed heartily.

"Lola, do you know what magnesium sulfate is?"

"No, though the name rings a bell."

"It's Epsom salt! That commercial is a bunch of hogwash!"

I had told her it was commercial hype. I passed along what the nutritionist said, and the customer was very appreciative. On TV, the product was $90 with a couple of free supplements thrown in with the order. They were selling a fifty-cent product for $90, so why not throw in a pacifier?

I went home that evening and appeased the fuzz in the back of my mind by checking the lawn products in the garage. Yep, there it was. A twenty-five pound bag of magnesium sulfate that I paid $9 for so my mother could grow healthy palm trees. Buyer beware.

God's Promise or Man's Opinion?

How many Christians would rather take the opinion of man over the Promise of God? Most of us have quoted the first part of Hosea 4:6 hundreds of times but never completed the entire Scripture:

> *"My people are destroyed for lack of knowledge: because thou hast rejected knowledge, I will also reject thee, that thou shalt be no priest to me: seeing thou hast forgotten the law of thy God, I will also forget thy children."*
>
> (Hosea 4:6 KJV)

We know quite well that ignorance can and often does become a detriment. Most of us who suffer for lack of knowledge never realize why we never learned what would have kept us out of our injurious predicament. The sheer truth is that first, we do not subject ourselves to an environment that presents the answers, and second, even if we are in an environment where knowledge is attainable, we refuse the information for whatever reason. More times than not, our refusal is based on tradition. We must ever be mindful that it is the tradition of men that makes the Word of God of no effect. Tradition has taught man to seek power and titles. Right or wrong, many folks cling to traditions for the sake of holding on to a heritage.

> *"And he said unto them, Full well ye reject the commandment of God, that ye may keep your own tradition. Making the word of God of none effect through your tradition, which ye have delivered: and many such like things do ye."*
>
> (Mark 7:9,13 KJV)

When I first began studying alternative healing, one of the first questions I was asked was, "Are you a doctor?" My response was, "No, of course not." Because I was not a medical doctor, some of my potential customers walked away. Ironically, most of these were highly-educated people with advanced stages of chronic diseases.

It is necessary for me to add that they were all Christians. How do I know? When I first began working in this industry, I only advertised on Christian radio, and it was the Christian community that responded. Yet, they turned their backs to God's Cure for healing, and many today have gone on to be with the Lord. I noticed, too, that the meek and humble blue-collar workers were pouring into our little shop and getting great results when using vitamins and herbs.

I am reminded of a relative of mine (We'll call her Gracie.) who is an educated woman in a very successful profession. By her own admission, she states, "I saw this uneducated, little cleaning lady about my age who looked the picture of health and got about like a teenager, and I had to ask her the secret to her fountain of youth." The woman told her that she had taken vitamins and herbs for many years. That set Gracie back; she took offense. "There's no way I'm going to let a cleaning woman look and live healthier than me, when I'm supposed to be so much more intelligent."

Knowledge is power only when it is put to use, for to know and not do is sin (James 4:17). The little cleaning lady was far wiser than many of the so-called elite because she applied the knowledge she had learned. Gracie, like many, had been told by the medical industry and their own private doctor that folks who practice alternative healing are quacks. They had heard that taking vitamins was a waste of money and only giving them expensive urine. They rejected the knowledge coming from God's Word and chose to retain heresy because the tainted information came from those who had medical degrees. It was of no interest to them that what we were teaching came from God's Word, even though they professed to be Christians. They were in the family of God, yet they chose to place their lives in the hands of those who rejected the solution that God had given them for a long life.

God has never failed, lied, deceived, disappointed, or denied those of us who are obedient to His Word, so tell me, why is it so difficult to allow God to lead and guide you? I know, there are some who may claim that God has let them down, but the context is that they were not operating in accordance with His spiritual Laws. Little do they know that they are responsible for their own letdown, simply because they rejected the knowledge of God's Word.

How Easy Is It to Get Off Medications?

How often have you heard folks say that they are waiting on God to heal them? The fact is, God has already healed them. To 'wait upon the Lord' means to act on what you know.

First and foremost, in today's medical industry, conscientious and compassionate physicians are aggressively studying and practicing alternative healing. Those physicians who are born-again Christians use conventional medicines as a last resort. Be determined to seek out a doctor who is licensed to practice both medical and nutritional healing. As a doctor friend of mine told me about ten years ago, "If we don't change over to nutritional healing, we're going to be out of business." The fact is, in today's market, those solely practicing conventional medications could even be looked upon as cynical.

How safe is it to get off conventional medications? Remove the fear, and you're two-thirds of the way home. Fear is what keeps most people on medication, and fear has torment. For over two decades, I have worked with doctors who advise against conventional medicines, except for infrequent cases. The body was manufactured from the dirt, and it takes the things that grow in the dirt to sustain that which comes from the dirt.

How easy is it to get off medications? In Matthew 9:29 (KJV), Jesus told His disciples, *". . . According to your faith be it unto you."* If we are to be followers of Christ, we need to observe and follow all of His teachings by faith. Let's face it: If we were operating in the God kind of faith, we would not have begun taking the harmful medications in the first place, because we would have been treating our bodies as the Temple of God, which it is, and we would consume a diet which would include only healthy and healing foods.

Recently, a woman came into the store looking for a solution to cancer. This woman could have been no older than forty-five. We've seen many customers healed of cancer simply by eating 70% raw vegetables and a few other natural products; everything we suggest comes from the Bible. She told me that she was taking three different blood pressure pills. The medications probably caused the cancer. In such a case, our first concern is strengthening the heart.

In the nineties, we learned the significance of CoQ10, and most folks were taking ten milligrams daily. When my dad was diagnosed with congestive heart failure and given only five days to live (He actually lived eight more years.), we administered 200 milligrams of CoQ10 daily, which we thought was an enormous dose, along with other necessary nutrients. In this woman's case, because more studies have been conducted on the importance of CoQ10, the recommended dosage for daily maintenance had recently been updated to thirty milligrams. I advised her to take 600 milligrams, along with a MCHA calcium, which is not just any calcium and magnesium, as previously stated, but the 'like-addressing-like' bioavailability nutrient most compatible with the body structure.

Not only does this supplement support the skeletal system but also the cardiovascular system:

"Calcium . . . is also important in the maintenance of regular heartbeat and in the transmission of nerve impulses. Calcium lowers cholesterol levels and helps prevent cardiovascular disease. . . . It may lower blood pressure and prevent bone loss associated with osteoporosis as well.

Research has shown that magnesium may help prevent cardiovascular disease, osteoporosis, and certain forms of cancer, and it may reduce cholesterol levels." (Prescription for Nutritional Healing 4th Edition, pp. 31, 36 by Phyllis A. Balch, CNC.

See also www.naturalnews.com/027392_magnesium_natural _disease.html)

What most folks don't understand is that if a product such as this formula is taken in a timely fashion, chances are remote that he or she would ever contract high blood pressure. This does not mean that MCHA or magnesium are the only nutrients needed to prevent high blood pressure, but they certainly play a major role. 600 milligrams of CoQ10 is a very healthy dose and only necessary for a short time, but in the case of a person taking three beta blockers (ouch!), it is quite advisable. Of course, we recommended that she consult with her doctor as a matter of protocol.

To get off the medication, though, many have taken their lives into their own hands, as Dr. Julian Whitaker recommended years ago in the first edition of his first book, *Reversing Heart Disease*. Today, Dr. Malkmus and many other honest and solid doctors are teaming up with their patients and getting them off synthetic medications. It isn't as difficult to stop taking medications as one may assume; however, it is extremely vital that the body is supported by healthy foods that do not obstruct or interfere with the healing process and quality nutrients necessary for healing. Change your diet, focusing on raw green vegetables. Exercise and get plenty of pure water and sunshine. Quote Scriptures on healing several times a day. It will only take about sixty days to give your body an overhaul; then see the new you!

It isn't always easy to help victims of conventional medications to understand the importance of taking a number of different herbs and vitamins. Many have been intimidated by friends, family, and sometimes their doctor. In such cases, it is imperative that the patient works with a physician who practices both alternative and conventional healing. If you are taking beta blockers, ask your doctor to work closely with you. Each case is different, and it could take as long as a year before your doctor permits you to totally discontinue the medications. Some medications, particularly beta blockers, if suddenly withdrawn from the body without sufficient nutritional support, will send the body into shock, especially if the body has not been provided with wholesome healing foods and exercise.

In my dad's case, we inundated his body with nutritional supplements; it only took us three days to take him off most of the meds. Mind you, since I was knowledgeable in the health field, we had no reservations, because we gave my dad only the best and finest nutrients to support the heart that doctors claimed would last only five more days. We proved the doctors wrong, and my dad lived another eight years. When he eventually passed over, it was because of renal failure, which resulted from the tremendous damage the heart medications had caused to his kidneys and liver.

Back to the woman taking the three beta blockers. I advise anyone taking synthetic medications to do a thorough background search to learn what side effects the medications are causing.

Conventional Medicine vs. Alternative Healing

In the article "Medicine's Use and Abuse" on the Alternative Information blog on Blogspot:

> "The study below Noted by JAMA, the Journal of the American Medical Association, shows exactly what I am saying. 300 Americans die each day from some effect from prescription drug use. 6,000 Americans, each day, suffer from very serious

ADVERSE REACTIONS from drugs. Remember all these are FDA approved drugs. From Aspirin that is estimated to kill 46 people a day to the more exotic drugs like Statins. Is this an epidemic? What would happen if this was caused by supplements?"

In the early '90s, one popular magazine published an article stating that the average lifespan of a medical doctor was fifty-seven years. Oddly, soon after, one of the most prominent doctors of our community was found in his automobile, dead of a heart attack. He died at the age of fifty-seven. This popular magazine also shared that over three million people are reportedly killed annually in hospitals as a result of malpractice, misdiagnosis, improper treatment through overdoses, incorrect medication, and even the amputation of the wrong leg or arm. There are documented cases where physicians have gone so far as to operate on the wrong patient and remove body parts. That's the history of our medical industry. There is a positive side to this story. Recently, someone inside the medical industry has taken the initiative help protect the patients. During a recent visit to the emergency room of two local hospitals, I witnessed attending nurses or medical assistants confirming the patient's identity prior to administering care or treatment. Without exception, the attendant verified the patient's name and date of birth prior to treatment. I was also pleased to see that these hospitals are prescribing vitamins. I seriously question, however, the quality of these vitamins since the patients are being treated by medical doctors who mainly prescribe conventional medications. I salute Dr. Julian Whitaker, a fierce but Godly medical doctor who was among the first, if not *the* first, medical doctor to expose the medical industry by stating outright that so-called chronic diseases can be reversed. In the introduction to the first edition of his book, *Reversing Heart Disease*, Dr. Whitaker wrote, "Do not put your life in the hands of a medical doctor," and he took one of the boldest positions ever taken in today's medical history. As I recall the story, he was examining a senior woman patient and was amazed at the youthfulness of her body. When he asked her secret, she told him that she had been taking vitamins and other supplements. It was at this point that Dr. Whitaker began to study alternative healing, and since that time, he has established what is probably the nation's greatest healing center.

I was at a tent meeting recently, and the minister shared information about a television show he had watched where a doctor stated something almost identical to a quote from Dr. Whitaker from years back. The minister went on to say that the doctor advised cancer patients to take extremely high levels of vitamin C to heal their cancer. I believe it was Dr. Whitaker who said that 20,000 milligrams of vitamin C had been proven to heal cancer, and he based this information on the research conducted by Dr. Linus Pauling, whom he highly esteemed. It's wonderful to see that God has raised up honest, God-fearing doctors who do not bow to Baal but are protective of God's people. Nutritional supplements are now mainstream, and it is also wonderful to see that many responsible citizens are taking charge of their own lives, as recommended by Dr. Whitaker.

Truth: The human body was created from the dirt.

Truth: The human body is designed to heal itself.

Deductive reasoning: If the body came from the dirt, then that which grows in the dirt will sustain that which comes from the dirt.

Menu:

> "And God said, Behold, I have given you every herb bearing seed, which is upon the face of all the Earth, and every tree, in the which is the fruit of a tree yielding seed; to you it shall be for meat."
>
> (Genesis 1:29 KJV)

Prescription:

> *"And by the river upon the bank thereof, on this side
> and on that side, shall grow all trees for meat, whose leaf
> shall not fade, neither shall the fruit thereof be consumed:
> it shall bring forth new fruit according to his months,
> because their waters they issued out of the sanctuary:
> and the fruit thereof shall be for meat, and the leaf thereof
> for medicine."*
>
> (Ezekiel 47:12 KJV)

I salute those brave and honest medical doctors, including
Dr. Whitaker, who have taken a stand by exposing the
unethical practices of our medical industry. Thank God that
these doctors choose to embrace the oracles of God and the
health of His people instead of falling prey to filthy lucre (1
Timothy 3:3). My sentiment is that God always has a ram in
the bush (Genesis 22:1-14). Yet medical doctors and hospitals
are the first choice for most of us experiencing discomfort or
disease. It's one thing to be tricked and not know it; it's another
to be tricked knowing it. Selah!

What Would Happen if All Corruption Was Exposed At Once?

The nation's most advertised multi-vitamin on television is
owned by a pharmaceutical company controlled by money. You
may say that all businesses are controlled by money; aren't they?
The answer is NO. Many businesses that operate with integrity
are motivated by results. In the health industry, businesses with
integrity are more concerned with saving lives than with stuffing
their stockholders' pockets. When a company knows the dangers
of releasing medications for public consumption, yet they
override these dangers — with the approval of the FDA — the
motive is money and the system is ill-wired.

> *"For the love of money is a root of all kinds of evil. Some people, eager for money, have wandered from the faith and pierced themselves with many griefs."*
>
> (1 Timothy 6:10 NIV)

This is the day when men call right wrong and wrong right. It is evident that the world's health system is controlled by heartless gougers whose only concern is padding their pockets and those of their colleagues. The health and lives of those being entrusted into their care mean absolutely nothing to them.

> *"Woe unto them that call evil good, and good evil; that put darkness for light, and light for darkness, that put bitter for sweet, and sweet for bitter!"*
>
> (Isaiah 5:20 KJV)

> *"For we know him that hath said, Vengeance belongs unto me, I will recompense, says the Lord. And again, The Lord shall judge his people. It is a fearful thing to fall into the hands of the living God."*
>
> (Hebrews 10:30-32 KJV)

We have been told time and time again that the Food and Drug Administration is controlled by monies funneled through it by the medical association and pharmaceutical companies. If the medical industry topples, so will the hospitals, clinics, doctors offices, medical supply companies, medical laboratories, mental health facilities, and so on down the line. God said that He would not destroy the land all at once but little by little until His people increased enough to take over:

> *"I will send my fear before thee, and will destroy all the people to whom thou shalt come, and I will make all thine enemies turn their backs unto thee. And I will send hornets before thee, which shall drive out the Hivite, the Canaanite, and the Hittite, from before thee. I will*

not drive them out from before thee in one year; lest the land become desolate, and the beast of the field multiply against thee. By little and little I will drive them out from before thee, until thou be increased, and inherit the land."
(Exodus 23:27-30 KJV)

I believe God is plucking the brows of corruption one hair at a time in the medical industry, because He has to avoid a world catastrophe. It is our job to continue praying that God will continue raising up honest physicians such as Dr. Julian Whitaker, Dr. George Malkmus, Dr. Don Colbert, and others who practice nutritional healing with integrity. We must pray, also, that God will send laborers to leaders of pharmaceutical companies, FDA regulators, and members of other entities who influence the medical industry so that they will give their lives to Christ and then work to heal the health industry.

Chapter Eight

HEALING AND FAITH

"But without faith it is impossible to please him: for he that cometh to God must believe that he is, and that he is a rewarder of them that diligently seek him."

(Hebrews 11:6 KJV)

Jesus Is Our Line Of Attack!

"I am the way, the truth, and the life."

(John 14:6 KJV)

I looked up 'way' in the thesaurus and found something that shook my world. Among its many meanings, the one that caused an explosion in my spirit was the phrase 'line of attack'! Saints of God, *Jesus is our line of attack!*

"And your feet shod with the preparation of the gospel of peace; Above all, taking the shield of faith, wherewith ye shall be able to quench all the fiery darts of the wicked."

(Ephesians 6:15-16 KJV)

Faith is our confidence that we will extinguish every single blow the devil sends our way, and Jesus is that Way, that certain, irrefutable victory.

"We having the same spirit of faith, according as it is written, I believed, and therefore have I spoken; we also believe, and therefore speak."

(2 Corinthians 4:13 KJV)

*"For with the heart man believeth unto righteousness;
and with the mouth confession is made unto salvation."*
(Romans 10:10 KJV)

You know whether or not a change has come over you. Everyone does. When you sincerely believe in your heart that you have been redeemed by the Blood of the Lamb and have a right standing with God because of the price that Christ Jesus paid at Calvary, then you're brand new! Your spirit has been changed into God's Likeness, and you are now capable of understanding God's Ways through His Word. You can now see yourself through the Eyes of God as His adorable child, and you are able to depend on Him totally. You value the fact that you are now legally entitled to every Promise spoken to you by your Father.

So, what do you do? You immerse yourself in your Father's Last Will and Testament (His Word, the Holy Scriptures), and learn every single provision of your inheritance, so that you don't miss an entitlement when making your claim. The Last Will and Testament was left for you, and you can enjoy all of its provisions because of your obedience. He believes in you, and He trusts that you will love, protect, covet, and adhere to His precious Provisions. This way, not only do you *believe* the inheritance is yours, but you become an active participant in exchanging the spiritual blessings for the manifest promises. You abide in Him, and now His Word abides in you.

You may ask yourself, "What are the heavenly blessings?" The answer in a nutshell is *all things*.

*"Blessed be the God and Father of our Lord Jesus Christ,
who hath blessed us with all spiritual blessings in
heavenly places in Christ."*
(Ephesians 1:3 KJV)

149

"Therefore let no man glory in men. For all things are yours; Whether Paul, or Apollos, or Cephas, or the world or life, or death, or things present, or things to come; all are yours, And ye are Christ's and Christ is God's."

(1 Corinthians 3:21-23 KJV)

Whatever promises you are able to receive as your very own, as an obedient child of God, they are yours.

". . . According to your faith be it unto you."

(Matthew 9:29 KJV)

It amazes me that so many Christians, having gone that first mile by confessing and receiving Jesus Christ as Lord and Savior, have never progressed to higher levels. The Bible teaches that we are to operate on a continual upward plane in our spiritual walk, from vessel to vessel, strength to strength, faith to faith, and glory to glory.

"For with the heart man believeth unto righteousness; and with the mouth confession is made unto salvation."

(Romans 10:10 KJV)

The first part of this Scripture tells us that if we confess with our mouth the Lord Jesus and believe with our heart that God raised Him from the dead, we will be saved. Being saved means that we are completely delivered from all of satan's tricks, including sickness. We were delivered by the Blood of Jesus at Calvary, but it takes our confessing it with our mouths before deliverance becomes a part of our lives. The entitlement is there, but it is up to us to make it personal.

"Surely he hath borne our griefs, and carried our sorrows: yet we did esteem him stricken, smitten of God, and afflicted. But he was wounded for our transgressions, he was bruised for our iniquities: the chastisement of our peace was upon him; and with his stripes we are healed."

(Isaiah 53:4-5 KJV).

The sin penalty was paid at Calvary, and included in this payment was sickness. We do not have to accept any sickness in our bodies. It is our responsibility to attend to our bodies, knowing that it is a place where God desires to dwell. God wants us to take this world by storm and then move upward to be with Him, as Enoch did. God does not make things complicated for His children. In fact, He declares that He takes the foolish or simple things of the world and causes the wise man to be confused:

> *"But God hath chosen the foolish things of the world to confound the wise; and God hath chosen the weak things of the world to confound the things which are mighty."*
> (1 Corinthians 1:27 KJV)

How difficult is it for you to say something — anything? How hard is it for you to make a statement? It's not difficult at all. You only have to open your mouth and speak. Remember, " . . . *with the mouth, confession is made unto salvation."* (Romans 10:10 KJV) When you speak, deliverance comes. Deliverance in this Scripture is to be set free from all of the subterfuges of satan, including sickness.

Recently, I was preparing to relax at home after work, and one of the first things I did was to slip out of my shoes. I noticed that my left foot felt a bit tight; surprisingly, once I took off my shoe, it began to swell quickly, as though it had been waiting for breathing room to thrust forward. My mind said *Wow!*, but my mouth said, "Oh, no, you lying vanity! I bind you, swelling, and command you to go, in the Name of Jesus!"

My mother happened to see, and instructed my little brother to get a rubbing agent. If you are past fifty, you know how conscious we must be of not treading on the feelings of our elderly parents. So, to prevent an argument, I permitted him to lightly dab the medicine on the top of my foot with a cotton ball. I quickly thanked him and said that the foot was healed. I took a few routine B6s, meant to protect the strength in my wrists; I am constantly pounding on the computer, and I knew that I would be spending several hours typing before retiring.

The next morning, my foot looked and felt as though nothing had ever been wrong. You may think that it was the rubbing agent, but I assure you, I did not allow my little brother to apply enough to make a difference. And it wasn't the vitamin B6; I was merely taking it for maintenance. What healed my foot were the words spoken from my mouth, commanding the swelling to leave and the healing to come forth.

More times than not, it is hopeless to attempt to explain God's Ways to a secular person because they will think you are being foolish. This is merely an attestation of God's Word. When I first got saved, my dear sister told folks that I had gone to La La Land, the loony farm — she thought I had lost my mind. What sane person, after all, would leave home, friends, family, and all personal belongings to go to a strange land, simply because God said *"Go"*?

Where I came from, everybody knew God. After all, they went to church on Sunday, said grace before meals, and taught the little ones to say the 'Now I lay me down to sleep' prayer before retiring for the night. What else was there to know about God, except that He made the trees and the bees and the fish in the seas?

At church on Sundays, the pastors never preached beyond David and Goliath, Daniel in the lion's den, and Peter walking on water. I've heard preachers giving 'glory' about an operation as though they should win a prize for having had their guts pieced back together. And they would protect fear in the pulpit as though it were a member of right standing with the church. Many sermons revolved around the six o'clock news, and that's Deuteronomy 28:15-68 if I ever heard it — gloom and doom. None of the messages delivered had any day-to-day application; they were just some good stories. So, in the realm of her understanding, it's clear to see why my sister thought I had lost my mind.

I remember a lady named Mrs. Betty who got filled with the Holy Ghost, and when she shared her experience with others, she became the neighborhood clown. Mrs. Betty went to the Holy Ghost Church, and Holy Ghost people were spooky. Everybody who wasn't filled with the Holy Ghost was afraid of the unknown. Now, I was becoming like Mrs. Betty, a straight-out fanatic. Why? Because I had the Holy Ghost. Like Mrs. Betty, I had what it took to speak sickness away. Mrs. Betty and I understood that with the Holy Ghost comes the power of God, and with God, all things are possible.

We must never expect a carnal-minded person to understand spiritual encounters. God warns us beforehand, *"But the natural man receiveth not the things of the Spirit of God: for they are foolishness unto him: neither can he know them, because they are spiritually discerned,"* (1 Corinthians 2:14 KJV). On many occasions, I have heard sick people say, "How can I say I'm healed when I have pain?" This is the natural mind speaking, and the natural mind cannot understand spiritual things.

In our church is a constant reminder that God is His Word (1 John 5:7). When we get to Heaven, we will be no closer to God than we are while reading His Word. That's why every Word of God must be treasured as a rare, newly-discovered gem. God says that His Word is health to all our flesh, which means that those who meditate on God's Word day and night, and obey it, should live in divine health. Only to the degree that we accept God's Word as truth will we fully enjoy His Promises. Yes, when we reach a level of maturation at which God's Word has ultimate influence over every situation in our lives, we will lack nothing. When we fully commit our bodies to God, surrendering to His holiness and healing, we will enjoy divine health. When the Word of God is the pivotal deciding factor for every decision we make, we will ask God for anything, and with all certainty, we will know that our prayers are answered. This place in our lives will find us bubbling over with joy, for it is the Father's good pleasure to give His children the desires of their hearts.

Many have not grasped the Truths of God's Word; others simply refuse to employ these Truths. God says, *"My people are destroyed for lack of knowledge: because thou hast rejected knowledge, I will also reject thee, that thou shalt be no priest to me: seeing thou hast forgotten the law of thy God, I will also forget thy children,"* (Hosea 4:6 KJV). How many times have I heard Christians repeat, *"My people are destroyed for lack of knowledge."* They quote the Scripture, but they only quote what they want to hear; or it could be that they only quote what the devil has allowed them to hear. The god of this world, satan, blinds the eyes of God's children and those who do not labor for an understanding of God's Word. The prophet Hosea includes in this Scripture the following warning: *"Because thou hast rejected knowledge, I will also reject thee, that thou shalt be no priest to me: seeing thou hast forgotten the law of thy God, I will also forget thy children."*

You have read the Word of God, you have heard the Word of God, you have even quoted the Word of God, yet you reject the Word of God. You allowed satan to steal it from your heart. It was not conducive to the manner in which you were living at the time, so you decided to cling only to that portion of the Word that you enjoyed. You squashed the portion that does not add flavor to your lifestyle. You treat the Word of God, which is your daily bread, as you would a buffet or a smorgasbord: Choose what your appetite savors and leave the rest. Take the part that promises to give you the desires of your heart, but leave the part where God's Word comes to teach, correct, instruct, convict, and transform.

> *"All scripture is given by inspiration of God, and is profitable for doctrine, for reproof, for correction, for instruction in righteousness."*
> (2 Timothy 3:16 KJV)

You forget these commands:

> *"For I am the LORD your God: ye shall therefore sanctify yourselves, and ye shall be holy; for I am holy."*
> (Leviticus 11:44 KJV)

And:

> *"Because it is written, Be ye holy, for I am holy."*
> (1 Peter 1:16 KJV)

Do you think that you can continue year in and year out committing the same sins and returning to God over and over, asking for forgiveness? This is a sure sign that you never really meant your confession of sorrow. You continue returning to the same filthy pig slop sins, never with the intentions of living pure and holy. That holiness stuff just doesn't fit into your agenda right now. No, no.

In Luke 7, Jesus was in Capernaum when a centurion's servant became ill, expecting to die. When the centurion heard about Jesus, he sent the elders of the Jews (those whom he felt Jesus would honor) to come to the house and heal his servant. When the elders explained how nobly the servant had performed, Jesus set out to go with them. However, before reaching the house, the centurion sent more of his representatives, who were also close friends, to tell Jesus that He had come far enough. The centurion felt that he was not worthy to have such a holy man enter his home. His words were,

> *"Lord, trouble not thyself for I am not worthy that thou shouldest enter under my roof. Wherefore neither thought I myself worthy to come unto thee: but say in a word, and my servant shall be healed."*
> (Luke 7:6-7 KJV).

Then he went on to let Jesus know that he understood the authority in which He walked, because he, too, was a man of authority.

"For I also am a man set under authority, having under me soldiers, and I say unto one, Go, and he goeth, and to another, Come, and he cometh, and to my servant, Do this, and he doeth it. When Jesus heard these things, he marveled at him, and turned him about, and said unto the people that followed him, I say unto you, I have not found so great faith, no, not in Israel."

(Luke 7:8-9 KJV)

God is omnipresent — He is everywhere at the same time. It is equally as effective for us to pray for the healing of an individual at a distance as it is to pray for one with whom we can see and touch. A few years ago, I prayed for a friend we will call Victoria who lives nearly four hundred miles from my home in Jacksonville, Florida. She was stricken with cancer, but when I cursed the root of that foul spirit of cancer, she was healed. Neither she nor I knew that the cancer had dried up at the time I prayed, but it wasn't many days later I learned that Victoria had gotten a report from her physician stating that she had been healed.

Just last night, one of my mother's friends, Ms. Katie, who lives 1,600 miles away, was on the phone with my mother, complaining of excruciating arthritic pain. I took the phone and asked her to place her hands over the area of pain. I prayed, commanding the spirit of arthritis with its pain to leave her body, and she said the pain left instantly. When I first began praying for others, I did not always get the results I desired so quickly. A few years later, people whom I had not seen in years began to visit me and share how I had prayed for them and how they were healed. Several years later, I noticed that nearly everyone with pain was healed when I prayed for them.

Never miss an opportunity to pray for someone, because God is always at work. He does the healing; we merely do the speaking. If you don't see results, keep praying anyway and never get discouraged. The more you practice, the more fluent you will become in operating in God's healing power.

Does this mean that everyone you pray for will get healed? No. My dad had been ill for a number of years before going home to be with the Lord. Needless to say, I prayed for him daily, but the end result was that his kidney failed and his body shut down.

My dad's brother was stricken with blindness. Sometimes we pray for our loved ones with such fervor that we absolutely feel that God has heard and answered our prayers. This was the case with my uncle. His wife and children gathered around him, and there was no question about the unity that existed in that room. We all had one common goal — that he would be restored. There was such power in that home that evening that I had no doubts that God would respond favorably, but God did not open his eyes.

We walk by faith, not by feelings. Because I had the 'feeling' that my dad and uncle would be healed meant nothing. How many times have I prayed for people and not 'felt' anything, yet God saw fit to heal them? I dare not theorize with finite humanistic reasoning. I've done that too many times in the past, only to have my theories proven wrong. God's Ways are not our ways.

I don't know why God did not heal my dad or uncle, but I know they are both at home with the Lord. Does this hinder me from moving forward? God forbid! In fact, it gives me more ammunition. If two out of ten do not get healed, I must work harder to keep a constant ratio or even make the results greater. We are never void of opportunities to prove God's healing Power in the lives of others.

Jesus marveled at the centurion's faith, because he had confidence that the power in Jesus' Words alone would heal his servant. Ms. Katie, whose arthritis I had prayed for over the phone, has visited our home and knows the life I live. When she heard me speak the Word of God, she had faith to believe that the arthritis would leave her body. The demonic spirit of infirmity obeyed her faith and the Word of God. Victoria, whose cancer had been healed through prayer, had never met me in person, but she certainly knew that we were both trusting the living Savior who had redeemed her from the curse of the law through His precious Blood, and through her belief, she was made whole. At the Name of Jesus, sickness and pain has to bow. Distance is no barrier to the healing power of God.

"Behold, the LORD's hand is not shortened, that it cannot save, neither his ear heavy, that it cannot hear."
(Isaiah 59:1 ASV)

My brother was shot by an erratic woman. When I got the call, my sister-in-law told me that doctors had given him a fifty-fifty chance of living. My sister in Florida telephoned me and asked if I wanted her to make plane reservations for me so that we could fly home to Indiana together to be at my brother's side. My response was, "You fly home; I'm going down on my knees."

I did just that. As I began to pray, I reminded God that His Word is Life, and when I sent it to my brother, life would have to spring forth. In the Name of Jesus, I took authority over death and every evil report, including spirits of doubt; then, I allowed the Holy Spirit to take charge by praying in the Spirit. God showed me two surgeons in the operating room with nurses by their side. The surgeons had on blue scrubs, and I could see them working. If you've had these types of visions before, you know that they don't last long but sort of flash by. I knew in my spirit that God was at work to save my brother. I labored in prayer, praying in tongues, until I got a breakthrough. Needless to say, my brother lived.

Location is everything for a prosperous business, but for God's business, location means nothing. Why? Because God is everywhere (see Psalms 139). God is never a distance away that He does not know what is going on in the life of His children, and His Power is not so frail that He is unable to deliver (Isaiah 59:1,

50:2). When we send His Word and release healing, the Power of God flows through the universe and attaches itself to its assigned target. The centurion understood the power that he possessed, and he recognized that Jesus possessed a far greater Power. It lives in us today, and when we become aware of the spiritual authority within ourselves through the Holy Spirit, we will speak life and health into any situation and know that we are victorious.

> *"But if the Spirit of Him who raised Christ Jesus from the dead dwells in you, He who raised Christ from the dead will also give life to your mortal bodies through His Spirit who dwells in you."*
>
> (Romans 8:11 NASB)

Words Bring Life

When the storm came, the disciples woke Jesus from a peaceful sleep so that He could speak to the storm. Jesus admonished them, *"Oh, ye of little faith."* Through your renewed mind, you now fully understand that the simplest way to receive those promises is through your confession.

> *"Ask and it shall be given unto you, seek and ye shall find, knock and the door shall be open."*
>
> (Matthew 7:7 KJV)

Genesis 2:7 says that God formed man from the dust of the ground and breathed into his nostrils the breath of life, *". . . and man became a living soul,"* (KJV). Some Torah translations render this, *" . . . and man became a talking spirit."*

> *"It is the spirit that quickeneth; the flesh profiteth nothing: the words that I speak unto you, they are spirit, and they are life."*
>
> (John 6:63 KJV)

159

In other words, when you speak the Word of God, you are creating life out of the wind of your body. When God blew spirit into you, He actually blew Himself into your body. Why do you think we can declare that, to paraphrase 1 John 4:4, 'Greater is He that is within me than he that is in the world'? Because it is God, Himself, living inside our bodies. The words you speak are bringing life because they are spoken out of your spirit.

Place your hand over your mouth and speak something, anything. Say it again. Say it again. What do you feel? Some say air; some, wind; others, breath. The fact is, they are all correct. What you feel coming from your mouth onto your hand is spirit. Spirit is life. God says, *"The words that I speak unto you, they are spirit, and they are life,"* (John 6:63). When the spirit is blown from your mouth, life enters into the atmosphere and flows into its targeted destination. You have begun to create! Create what? That depends upon you. Whatever words project from your mouth, the manifestation of those words produce life, and the fruit is either death or life, based on what you have chosen to speak.

Please understand, because we are talking spirits, and because everything is formed in the spirit before it manifests itself in the natural, we are able to confess any situation into our lives. Our words have the same creative ability as God's Words, because He made us in His image, to look and act like Him. As such, we can speak deliverance in every area into our lives.

During my stay in Indiana, shortly after I left my brother's home, God provided me with a home of my own. The seven-room house was a miracle, but it required lots of work. I was not only grateful for the home but equally excited to have total control over its renovations. The master bedroom was upstairs, and part of the renovation included the installation of a full bathroom. The work had not begun, but I had placed a bed upstairs to isolate myself from any distracting noise.

I recall a specific morning on which I was trying to get up and begin my routine day. To my amazement, I could not move my right side. I tried to move my leg, but it was paralyzed. I tried to stand, but there was no life or movement from my waist down on the right side. I did not attempt to rationalize what had happened to me, but with all confidence, I focused on a verse that belonged to me:

> *"For verily I say unto you, That whosoever shall say unto this mountain, Be thou removed, and be thou cast into the sea, and shall not doubt in his heart, but shall believe those things which he saith shall come to pass, he shall have whatsoever he saith. Therefore, I say unto you, What things soever ye desire, when ye pray, believe that ye receive them, and ye shall have them."*
> (Mark 11:23-24 KJV)

I was certain that whatever I asked God for would be mine. Right then, I needed a healing, so it was my responsibility to exercise the power within me and remind God of His Promises pertaining to healing. The first words spilling out of my mouth were, "I bind you, spirit of paralysis, in the Name of Jesus, and command you to leave my body!"

I lay back down and began to very authoritatively quote healing Scriptures, one after another, while focusing on points throughout my leg and body. "I plead the Blood of Jesus through my body. Father, I thank You that Your Word is health to all my flesh. Thank You for paying for my sins and sicknesses, and, therefore, I am healed by Your Blood. Thank you that you took sickness away from me . . . " I repeated healing Scripture after healing Scripture for perhaps two hours.

I wanted to find someone to agree with me for my healing; the first person who came to mind was my mother. But I immediately cancelled the thought. As recently as the year before last, even

LOLA HARDAWAY

in her improved state, I would tell friends and family not to tell Mother if they were not feeling well, because she would have them dead and buried before the conversation was over. Thank God she's better today!

My dad would have prayed for me, period. After the prayer, he would not only listen to Mother but also concur and then conform to every word she spoke, "Call the doctor. Call an ambulance. Call the fire department. Where on Earth can we find a wheelchair?" You get the picture.

After a bit of pondering, I thought of Linda. While in California, she and I had become great friends. Linda was completely sold out to God, and as I knew from her conversation and lifestyle, she was on the same wavelength as me when it came to exercising faith. I telephoned her, and we prayed the prayer of agreement for my healing. I slept quite well awhile longer, but when I awoke, the paralysis was still there. I kept speaking the Word of God, and finally, after another few hours, I felt the spirit leap out of my body. I jumped up and felt no aftereffects — no weakness, no lingering pain, nothing. The spirit of infirmity was gone.

> *"But in all things approving ourselves as the ministers of God, in much patience, in afflictions, in necessities, in distress."*
> (2 Corinthians 6:4 KJV)

> *"Cast not away therefore your confidence, which has great recompense of reward."*
> (Hebrews 10:35 KJV)

> *"My brethren, count it all joy when ye fall into divers temptations; Knowing this, that the trying of your faith worketh patience. But let patience have her perfect work, that ye may be perfect and entire, wanting nothing."*
> (James 1:2-4 KJV)

Many Christians will ask God for a healing or any other blessing, as these principles apply, and because the answer is not immediate, they give up. Little do they know, as heirs to the Kingdom of God, our prayers are being processed. Imagine a roadway sign waving in the heavens, "Patient, Prayers Being Processed."

Read Daniel 10 for the complete story, but here's the short version: After Daniel had fasted for twenty-one days, the Angel of the Lord visited him and said,

> ". . . Fear not, Daniel, for from the first day that you set your mind and heart to understand and to humble yourself before your God, your words were heard, and I have come as a consequence of [and in response to] your words. But the prince of the kingdom of Persia withstood me for twenty-one days. Then Michael, one of the chief [of the celestial] princes, came to help me, for I remained there with the kings of Persia. Now I have come to make you understand what is to befall your people in the latter days, for the vision is for [many] days to come."

(Daniel 10:12-14 AMP)

We must understand that there are ongoing activities in the spirit realm, and satan and his host are forever battling to impede and even stop the success of the saints. In Daniel's case, there was a twenty-one-day wait. Some of you have been waiting far longer than that to receive answers to your prayers; it is an indication that God wants you to co-labor with Him.

Michael is the chief war Angel who assisted Daniel in battle. Angels are sent to help those of us who are to receive salvation (see Hebrews 1:14). As explained by Michael, his job was to retrieve Daniel's words and present them before the Father for execution. Are you sending up words to God?

"Bless the Lord, ye his angels, that excel in strength, that do his commandments, harkening unto the voice of his word."

(Psalm 103:20 KJV)

All too often, we are too impatient, not allowing God's Angels to work on our behalf. All too often, we fail to fast and pray so that we can receive directives from God. I recall one morning bright and early; I was awakened so sweetly by the bright Florida sun shining through my patio window. As I lay with my eyes shut, basking in the heat from the sun and meditating on how wonderful I felt, I had a closed-eyed vision of the word 'fenugreek'. It is a leafy plant native to India and the Middle East. This was during my startup days in the health industry, and although I did not know what health benefits fenugreek held, I knew that it was an herb that God was instructing me to take. It was His way of preventing diabetes from manifesting itself in my body, and He knew exactly what I needed. Had I not lived a life of prayer, I would not have been able to hear from God, and satan may have gained a stronghold over my body.

God's Word requires action. A person who gives up on God will never enjoy the exceedingly abundant life God has planned for him or her. Awhile back, one of our customers brought his X-rays into the store for advice. His entire upper torso was overtaken with cancer. The very first thing we did, of course, was to pray and put an axe to the root of every cancer cell in his body. I explained to him that the body heals itself, and most cancers result from poor diets.

When we discontinue eating foods that feed the disease and eat only what the body is made of, the healing process begins. We gave him super green foods, such as wheat grass and barley, along with the daily nutritional supplements that are recommended for foundational support. We also supplied him with the greatest herbal cancer destroyer and other nutrients to support the body's pH, cellular balance, and immune system.

The healing process had begun. This customer was diligent. I speculated that the cancers should be gone in six months, but to rebuild strong cells, he should follow the regimen for twelve to eighteen months.

The customer, though disciplined, was a veteran, and doctors from the VA Hospital were encouraging him to have surgery. I could tell that fear was beginning to set in. After about three months, he brought in a new set of X-rays, but they were not legible. These X-rays were taken from a strangely different position, and neither the healing process nor the cancer, which had been quite prevalent on the first X-rays, could be detected. It was impossible to determine anything on the body from the new X-rays, so I knew something was going on. Also, I could tell that the customer was becoming more and more fearful. According to him, the doctors at the VA Hospital prescribed conventional medications, but he took only the nutritional supplements. The customer was also eating 70% raw vegetables and fruits, which included daily juicing.

Finally, after four months, his doctors convinced him that he could no longer wait for the surgery. Understandably, veterans are treated at no cost as a part of their medical benefits, and they don't want to do anything to upset the doctors or infringe upon their relationship with them. According to him, when the doctors performed the surgery, they found that his entire upper torso was healed of all cancers, except for a portion about the size of a dime. They were so amazed that they called in specialists from other parts of the country to examine the results. He said that all the nurses at the hospital were calling him "The Miracle Man."

He never felt pain while in recovery for two hours; he was fully alert and comfortable. He was home shortly, with absolutely no downtime. When he reported back to me, he expressed sincere regret for not waiting out the six months. It is clear, however, that though this patient operated with a measure of fear — I call it 'weary flesh', but someone else developed a great acronym, 'False Evidence Appearing Real' — The bottom line is that God met him where he was and gave him complete victory.

Saints of God, we must understand that when God's children exhibit less than wholeness, greatness, and perfection to the world, it is an insult to God, who has given us every provision for wellness and prosperity. He is returning to the Earth to pick up His body of believers who have no spots, wrinkles, illnesses, sicknesses, or infirmities; we must become a violent church and take what belongs to us!

> *"And from the days of John the Baptist until now the kingdom of heaven suffers violence, and the violent take it by force."*
>
> (Matthew 11:12 NKJV)

Suppose I had fainted the first five hundred or thousand times I spoke God's Word and then stopped. What do you suppose would have happened? Because I carry the Name of Jesus; because I realize and acknowledge that He has given me the authority to cast out sickness in His Name, I refuse to give in to the devil. Hallelujah! Jesus is our LINE OF ATTACK! I'm shouting these words even as I stroke the keyboard, and you ought to join me. Let's say it: JESUS IS OUR LINE OF ATTACK! Now, personalize it and shout it again: JESUS IS *MY* LINE OF ATTACK! If I were you, I'd shout Scripture over and over again until every single demon assigned to your body runs as far away from you as it can. Faith is a way-maker, and Jesus is the Way!

> *"I am the way, the truth, and the life."* (John 14:6 KJV)
> *"Take heed, brethren, lest there be in any of you an evil heart of unbelief, in departing from the living God."*
>
> (Hebrews 3:12 KJV)

I've often looked at my life and analyzed myself, noticing when things were not advancing for the benefit of the Kingdom, and I have said, "If I'm not moving forward, then I'm in a backsliding state." God promises that He takes us from faith to faith, and by studying, listening, and trusting the Word of God, we see how God prompts us to larger and greater situations for advancement. He takes us from strength to strength for greater boldness, so that our lives repel, more and more, the suggestions presented to us that counter God's Word. He takes us from vessel to vessel; we pull off the old skins and drink of the new wine. Finally, He takes us from glory to glory, bringing His undeniable Presence into our lives, changing us inwardly into perfection, projecting His radiance on the outside, and causing the manifestation of His power to change the lives of others.

You Need Some Dynamite!

> *"But you shall receive power [dunamis: dynamite miraculous power, force, might, strength, enabling power through the Holy Spirit] when the Holy Spirit has come upon you."*
>
> (Acts 1:8 AMP)

This power transforms — trust me! We are not just small firecracker-sized explosions of power, but instead we hold dynamic, seismic, and cataclysmic power. This power is so great that when it comes upon us nothing is impossible — and everything is possible. It is an earth-shattering, limitless, unceasing, consistent, unending availability of mega-wattage divine power that rattles the world around you. Have you experienced the kind of power in your life that shakes, influences, moves, and transforms? You will need it if you want to leave a legacy for future generations.

I was shopping at a department store one afternoon when the clerk recognized me and came over to give me a hug. "Do you remember me?" she asked.

"I know your face, but I can't place the name," I replied. I see so many people on a day-to-day basis, and I have yet to accomplish the art of memorizing every customer's name.

"I was in your store; I had a mass on my breast. You prayed for me, and when I went to the doctor, it was gone." I thanked her for sharing the story, but she went on. "That's not all; I sent my friend to see you, because she had cancer. When she went back to the doctor, the cancer was gone."

I hear these kinds of stories quite frequently. One little lady came into the store and told me, "I was here awhile back, and I had *two* tumors. When you prayed for me, both of the tumors left. The doctors could not find them at all!"

I love God's people so much that I never want to pass up an opportunity to see the Power of God at work in their lives, and God wants *you* to feel the same way. What better place is there to begin than to open your mouth and bind the infirmity in your own body? Speak divine health over your body every day, and if by chance a spirit of infirmity creeps its way through your flesh, it must back out because your body will repel against it. Practice speaking the Word of God. Practice calling on the Name of Jesus, because He is our 'line of attack', and you will see miracle after miracle in your life and in the lives of others.

Children Look Like Their Parents, Don't They?

We presently reside in two worlds, the natural world and the spirit world, and this is an inescapable reality. Those of us who have been Christians for any length of time know that we are composed of three parts, or tripartite beings: spirit, soul, and body. 'Spirit' is who we are, 'soul' is our mind and emotions, and 'body' is simply a boarding place, housing everything that makes us work. God takes pleasure in calling our body His Temple.

> *"What? know ye not that your body is the temple of the Holy Ghost which is in you, which ye have of God, and ye are not your own?"*
>
> (1 Corinthians 6:19 KJV)

The temple is a most sacred sanctuary, built to worship God and to house the Oracles of the Most High. After all, we are the Body of His Son, Christ Jesus, who purchased us with the price of His precious Blood and left us with the Holy Spirit to perform our earthly assignments through Him. Our spirit is the real person. This is the part of man which is made in God's Image, which means we look like Him, and in God's Likeness, which means that we have the capacity to behave like Him.

> *"And God said, Let us make man in our image, after our likeness . . ."*
>
> (Genesis 1:26 KJV)

Did God not tell us to have dominion over every creeping thing that crept over the face of the Earth?

> *"...and let them have dominion over the fish of the sea, and over the fowl of the air, and over the cattle, and over all the earth, and over every creeping thing that creepeth upon the earth."*
>
> (Genesis 1:26 KJV)

Yes, He did. Did God not tell us to take the land wherever the soles of our feet tread?

> *"Every place whereon the soles of your feet shall tread shall be yours from the wilderness and Lebanon, from the river, the river Euphrates, even unto the uttermost sea shall your coast be."*
>
> (Deuteronomy 11:24 KJV)

Yes, He did. You may ask, how is it possible that we are made to look like God? The answer is very simple: *"God is a Spirit . . ."* (John 4:24 KJV) Just as God is a Spirit, we, too, are spirits. God is not only a Spirit, but also our Creator and Father. The Bible tells us that as He is, so are we. As Creator, God has wondrously and marvelously made and created each of us to be as He is, yet with distinct traits, as evidenced by the individualism of each man's fingerprints, or more recently, DNA. As He is, so are we. It is my belief that when we get to Heaven and see God, each one of us will look just like Him. I believe this is the reason God was so emphatic when He commanded man not to make a graven image of Him.

> *"Thou shalt not make unto thee any graven image, or any likeness of any thing that is in heaven above, or that is in earth beneath, or that is under the earth."*
>
> (Exodus 20:4 KJV)

The word 'image' here is *pecel* (pronounced peh-sel, Strong's 1788, 6459), meaning 'idol'. God is our all-powerful Father, and nothing is too difficult for Him. For Him to make every one of His children to look like Him, in my opinion, is elementary. After all, children are supposed to look like their parents. God is our Father, and He is just that great.

God gave me the most revelatory experience some years back. It was seven in the morning, and I was at home in East Los Angeles watering my lawn before going to work. A stranger walked past, spoke kindly to me, and then kept walking down the long, long block. I saw him about three Chicago blocks away as he neared the corner, but I never noticed him return to my house a few minutes later. I was preoccupied with my lovely lawn when suddenly he was on my walkway and marching up to me to ask, "Pardon me, ma'am, are you James and Rose's daughter?"

I was taken aback. I had no relatives in Los Angeles, and other than the few folks I had met and perhaps shared a few family stories with while there, I knew absolutely no one who knew my family. Even the stories I may have shared could not have imparted any physical resemblance I held to my parents. Nonetheless, it was clear that this man knew my parents. I was a bit slow to answer, but certainly not out of fear, "Yes, sir, I am." I was so surprised that someone in Los Angeles, California, knew my parents who lived way back in Indiana. "Who are you?"

To make a long story short, this man was my third-grade teacher's brother, who knew my parents from back in East Chicago, Indiana. I had never seen him before in my life, not even as a child, but because my DNA was a blend of James and Rose's, there was no mistake about who my parents were. I was on the other side of the country, more than two thousand miles from home, and my features so strikingly resembled my parents' that he recognized me immediately. There was no guessing the roots of my identity; I looked just like my parents because they conceived me. I was born into the family of James and Rose.

When God blew spirit into Adam, He blew the Life of Himself into man, creating His offspring. The same Breath that God used to create the world was used to form man, and it was called the Breath of Life. Because God is Spirit, and it was a spiritual impartation that He blew into man to reproduce life, then we can easily understand the translation *"man became a talking spirit,"* at the time of Creation. We can also interpret this saying as, *"man became a speaking life-force."* God's only Instrument of Creation was Spirit, or Words coming from Spirit. His Word is Spirit and Life (see John 6:63). Therefore, at the time God created man, man became a 'talking spirit', forcing life into all that was breathed from him.

> *"Beloved, now are we the sons of God, and it doth not yet appear what we shall be: but we know that, when he shall appear, we shall be like him, for we shall see him as he is."*
> (1 John 3:2 KJV)

When we see God, we shall be like Him. I believe that every eye that looks upon God will look just like their Father who is God, because His Word says that as He is, so are we. God made us in His Image, which means that He made us to look like Him. He made us in His Likeness, so we are created to act like Him. Doesn't every father, if he's honest, want his child to follow in his footsteps and act like him? Of course he does, if he is a loving, caring father. As such, if God did not want us to look and act like Him, why would he call us His children? Nowhere in the Bible does God refer to us as His adults. He admonishes us to get off the milk and mature in His Word, but in His eyes, we are, "My little children . . ."

NOWHERE IN THE BIBLE DOES GOD CALL US HIS ADULTS

Why? One reason is because He wants us to obey and be taught by Him. All children must be taught. All children require a plausible example to follow. Also, proud parents want their children to look like them. "Yeah, that's my handsome son," or "See my beautiful daughter, spitting image of her Father." Can't you hear His proud heartbeat? Why do you think God placed such a strong desire in the fathers to want their children to look and behave like them, especially the male child who will carry on his name? When Jesus taught His disciples to pray, He prayed that God's Kingdom would come to this Earth and everything on Earth would be just as it is in Heaven, including God's Image and Likeness reflected in His earthly children.

If you ever once were bothered by the way you look — cheer up; your redemption draws nigh. You are beautifully, marvelously, and wonderfully created in your Father's Image.

God would not have it any other way. He is so powerful that He can do anything, and He has made you in His Image to look and act like Him. This means that you, too, can do anything through Christ Jesus, through whom the worlds were made.

> *"Hath in these last days spoken unto us by his Son, whom he hath appointed heir of all things, by whom also he made the worlds."*
>
> (Hebrews 1:2 KJV)

Our spirit is capable of operating on the same level as Jesus, provided our soul is renewed and made alive through God's Word. The Apostle Paul begs or beseeches us to offer up ourselves as a living sacrifice, holy and acceptable unto God. He goes on to plead that we are not conformed to this world but that we are transformed by the renewing of our minds. Our minds are changed to act like God when we plant His Word, which is Spirit, into our souls.

IT IS FATAL TO BE CLASSIFIED AS A CHRISTIAN AND NEGLECT GOD'S WORD, WHICH IS GOD.]

> *"For there are three that bear witness in heaven: the Father, the Word, and the Holy Spirit; and these three are one."*
>
> (1 John 5:7 KJV)

It is spiritual suicide to go to war and forget your ammunition. That's what it means to become a Christian but to forsake spending time with God each day. Unless you practice God's Word, it is impossible to become transformed. Prior to getting saved or becoming born again, we who were living in pleasure were considered dead. In 1 Timothy 5:6 it says, *". . . and she that lives in pleasure is dead while she lives."* I call it "dead man walking."

*"It is the spirit that quickened; the flesh profited nothing:
the words that I speak unto you, they are spirit, and they
are life."*

(John 6:63 KJV)

When we immerse ourselves in the Word of God, because
His Word is Spirit, we are joining His Spirit with our spirit and
producing His Life in us. The more we embrace and meditate
on His Word and permit it to flow from our mouths, the more
we align our lives with it and allow it to transform us, and the
stronger and more creative our words become. The more we feast
upon His Word, the more our words are empowered through the
Spirit of Might. We speak a thing, and we create what we speak.
Our words, which are spirit, become life. As He is, so are we. It
is the renewed or developed spirit of man that causes man to
operate on the same level as Jesus operated, and even beyond.
I remind you of what Jesus said: *". . . the works that I do shall he
do also, and greater works than these shall he do, because I go unto my
Father."* (John 14:12 KJV)

I'm sure Jesus never so much as caught a common cold. The
short years of Jesus' earthly ministry were meant to demonstrate
to us that we could be totally perfect; *"Be ye therefore perfect, even
as your Father which is in heaven is perfect,"* (Matthew 5:48 KJV). I
know you've been hearing from pulpits all over the world that
no one can be perfect. Hold on just a little bit and I will make it
easy for you to be perfect, but first you must learn to always agree
with what God has written in His Word about you. That's simply
another definition of the term 'faith': to align yourself with all
that God says about you and trust Him wholly to bring what He
says into fruition.

*"Being confident of this very thing, that he which has
begun a good work in you will perform it until the day
of Jesus Christ."*

(Philippians 1:6 AKJV)

Why do we have to accept the unsubstantiated hypothesis that we must get sick? God promises that He will perform the good work that He began in us. When God created man, He said that His work was very good.

In order for Him to perform the good work that He began in us, He will bring us to complete perfection when we honor, acknowledge, and trust in Him. Why do some people accept the common opinion that we must die with some sort of disease? These forged propagandas have brought on millions, perhaps billions, of sicknesses and deaths, and they are totally contrary to God's Promises. God said that He took sickness away from us (Exodus 23:25), which means that we are to walk in divine health. When we study and meditate on God's Word, it becomes health to all of our flesh (Proverbs 4:20-22), as we obey what we read. So, in the event that satan has attempted to introduce illnesses into your body, as we meditate on the Word of God, it will swiftly eradicate the sickness. Our responsibility is to keep the faith. Trust in the Lord with all your heart and do not lean to your own understanding (Proverbs 3:5). Losing faith is losing trust in God, and God is painfully hurt when we let Him down.

Being told that you are not capable of becoming what God wants you to become is just another trick from the devil, and this deception has lived too long. Being told that you cannot have what God has promised in His Word is robbery. I've heard many say, "It's hard to obey the Word." My immediate retort is, "Are you a sinner?" I then proceed to explain that Jesus said in Matthew 11:30 that His yoke is easy and His burden is light. Good understanding gives favor, but the way of the transgressor is hard (Proverbs 13:15). Thus, when you find it difficult to obey the Word of God, it is because you are living the life of a transgressor. Selah!

Christ Jesus came to demonstrate to us that we can and should perform great works and bring the Body of Christ to His fullness. Romans 8:11 teaches us that the same Spirit that raised Jesus from the grave lives in us. That same Spirit joined with Mary's and formed eternal life in her womb. When permitted, it will produce eternal life in you. Man is in an identity crisis. Unfortunately, man, a spirit being, has been so indoctrinated into the natural world that he must begin almost from scratch to learn his true identity.

MAN, A SPIRIT BEING, HAS BEEN SO INDOCTRINATED INTO THE NATURAL WORLD THAT HE MUST BEGIN ALMOST FROM SCRATCH TO LEARN HIS TRUE IDENTITY.

If we want to triumph in the spirit realm as well as in the natural world, it is prudent for us to learn to cooperate confidently with both worlds. Based on the laws we choose to apply to our lives, we will either be victims or victors in these two worlds. The decision is ours.

Chapter Nine

DEPRESSION

"Anxiety in the heart of man causes depression, But a good word makes it glad."

(Proverbs 12:25 NKJV)

Just as Jesus prayed for Peter that his faith would not fail, He is also praying for you and me: *"It is Christ that died, yea rather, that is risen again, who is even at the right hand of God, who also maketh intercession for us."* (Romans 8:34 KJV; see also Hebrews 7:25)

Have you ever felt gloom and doom because things did not go your way? This is satan leading you into depression. Have you ever felt as though you wanted to hide from the world because you failed at a project? Did depression swarm around your mind because you wanted a special trip or venture but the money or resources weren't there? Perhaps you got a foreclosure notice because you did not have the money to pay your mortgage. Perhaps you were in a near-fatal accident and had to have one of your limbs amputated, or maybe you were diagnosed with a terminal illness. Now you have to settle for death because that's what the doctor said.

Do you think any of these misfortunes is a reason to become depressed? These are all tricks from satan. Have you been depressed because of someone else's ill-fortune? It could even have been the loss of a loved one, a divorce, or perhaps a miscarriage. There are times when grieving is justified, but how long does it last? These are all ill-feelings, and, in some cases, if you want to brood for a moment, you may be entitled. But for the sake of trusting God, don't be tricked into permitting satan to control your life under any circumstance. Emotions are controllable, and it's up to you to decide how long you will allow sadness to rule in your life.

"For who has known the mind of the LORD that he may instruct Him? But we have the mind of Christ."
(1 Corinthians 2:16 NIV)

When we have the mind of Christ, we are able to program our emotions and control what is dictating our responses. We accept plausible challenges and seek solutions. We never allow circumstances to dictate how we are to act or react, which means that we do not 'internalize' our circumstances. Know that you are in control and that you are being guided by the Holy Spirit. Often, ill-feelings are far-fetched and demonic, and they are tricks from the devil! Notice that I said ill-*feelings*. Faith is faith, and feelings are feelings. One has nothing to do with the other. If ever you were depressed, satan has assigned his wicked little demons of depression to swarm around your head and whisper misery and even death into your ears.

Oppression and depression are closely related — though the former is characterized just below the latter — and many sicknesses are rooted in these diseases. Depression has been known to grow so deeply that it is not uncommon for a depressed person to commit suicide.

A few weeks before Christmas, my niece (whom I do not see very often) came to visit. I asked if she was looking forward to celebrating Christmas. Her response was, "I don't celebrate Christmas."

"Why?" I asked, quite surprised, as my mind flashed back to a few splendid holidays we had shared when she was a child. "Is it because Christmas is close to your dad's birthday?" Her dad, my younger brother, had gone to be with the Lord.

"That, and also because this is when my sister passed away."

I could not believe what came from her mouth. I could not recall the exact year her sister had passed, but it hadn't been too long after my brother's accidental death, and that was in 1983, nearly thirty years before!

"That's a demon of grief," I told her, "for *satan* has tricked you into oppression at the most glorious time of the year. That demon has succeeded in denying you the joy of celebrating the birth and life of our Savior Jesus Christ. Why can't you see what he's doing?"

Broken Hearts Are Real

> *"The sacrifices of God are a broken spirit; a broken and contrite heart, O God, you will not despise."*
> (Psalm 51:17 NIV)

> *"He heals the brokenhearted and binds up their wounds."*
> (Psalm 147:3 NIV)

According to a study conducted at UCLA, a broken heart actually hurts, physically. *Proceedings of the National Academy of Sciences* reported that scientists at UCLA had discovered a gene linked to both physical and emotional or social pain. ". . . a variation in the mu-opioid receptor gene (OPRM1), often associated with physical pain, is related to how much social pain a person feels in response to social rejection."

A group of participants underwent a series of tests involving social rejection. Professor Naomi Eisenberger, the study's co-author, said of the results, "Individuals with the rare form of the pain gene, who were shown in previous work to be more sensitive to physical pain, also reported higher levels of rejection sensitivity and showed greater activity in social pain-related regions of the brain when they were excluded."

Anyone who has ever experienced the emotional pain of rejection or loss already knows this to be true, of course. As Christians, we know that the painful reality of a 'broken heart' is not the end of our lives. Jesus proclaimed in Luke 4:18 (NKJV), *"The Spirit of the Lord is upon Me, because He has anointed Me to preach the Gospel to the poor; He has sent Me to heal the brokenhearted . . ."*

During those times when we may feel sick at heart, we learn to lean on the Comforter, the Holy Spirit. It is so true that He gives us peace that passes understanding. In fact, during such times, we become more sensitive to our need for God and are open to His Touch in our lives. If ever you experience emotional pain or rejection, you understand that what you feel is real. There is a physical hurt, but God is right there waiting for you to call upon Him to bring healing to your broken heart. He never leaves you or forsakes you.

Getting back to my niece: For a person to remain hurt, oppressed, and dejected for almost three decades is a sin. Grief can be a lingering demon, and as Christians we must be able to discern its presence.

There are two types of depression, endogenous and reactive. I believe that my niece was suffering from reactive depression, because emptiness and the inability to experience pleasure seemed to trail her over the years. This familiar spirit of grief would rear its ugly head each year at Christmas. It had won over her joy and happiness at a time when she should have been so happy. It had lingered too long.

As stated earlier, oppression is a disease characterized just below depression, and various sicknesses are ingrained in these diseases. One simple act of binding those demons and commanding them to leave brought a joy over my niece, and her eyes were opened. I believe that depression in this instance had begun through rejection. Her father passed away when she was young, and it opened the door for rejection, which, in turn, opened the door for rebellion and bitterness, causing her to pull away. In this case, also, the priesthood of the family was no longer in place; her mother had to rule the house but proved overly permissive, which resulted in improper discipline. All of these spirits are interrelated.

> *"In whom the god of this world hath blinded the minds of them which believe not, lest the light of the glorious Gospel of Christ, who is the image of God, should shine unto them."*
>
> (2 Corinthians 4:4 KJV)

The god of "this" world is satan. Notice how he blinds the thought processes of the unbeliever. The root of the word 'blind' in Strong's Concordance 5185 is taken from *typhloo* (tuflo-o) and means:

1) to raise a smoke, to wrap in a mist
   a) to make proud, puff up with pride, render insolent
   b) to be puffed up with haughtiness or pride
2) to blind with pride or conceit, to render foolish or stupid
   a) beclouded, besotted

In other words, the sinner whose mind is blinded is walking in an atmosphere of demonic smog. He or she is being tricked and deceived by an arrogant and haughty spirit of pride, which comes before a fall (Proverbs 16:18). Shame and strife also follow one whose eyes are blinded by satan. Now that this person has permitted the devil to take control, he or she is stripped of all confidence and dignity and swims in a river of shame and depression. The etymologist even goes so far as to say that a person whose mind is blinded by *satan* is rendered 'foolish or stupid'.

Pride is idolatry, the worship of oneself, and it causes one to become puffed up and deluded, having projected a false image of oneself. Destruction comes, and when it does, satan assigns tiny snake-like demons to throng around the head, day and night, speaking embarrassment, self-hatred, and even suicide. There is no chance for light or joy to enter in because satan has blocked all entrances to the mind.

> *"On that day, I will banish the names of the idols from the land, and they will be remembered no more," declares the LORD Almighty. "I will remove both the prophets and the spirit of impurity from the land."*
> (Zechariah 13:2 NIV)

If you find yourself depressed, it is because your access to the Throne of God has been blocked by demons. Chief demon satan makes you feel self-pity, and all self-esteem vanishes. He doesn't want you to enjoy life, and he presents every reason for you to believe that you cannot and will not succeed. He places a dark shadow in your mind about God, with doubt, unbelief, distrust, and other blinding propositions.

Patricia Nevins, RN, writing for Livestrong.com, says that depression causes, ". . . neurological changes in the brain resulting in mental, emotional, and physical changes . . . Depression weakens the immune system, particularly natural killer T-cells which help protect the body from carcinogens (cancer-causing agents). A weakened immune system also affects the body's inflammatory response. The NIHM reports that this physical effect of depression has been related to an increased incidence of osteoarthritis, asthma, heart disease, and autoimmune disorders." (http://www.livestrong.com/article/28799-depression-affect-body/#ixzz1GErxYsD3)

When one undergoes neurological changes in the brain resulting from depression, it follows that the spirit of suicide enters. These are also mind-controlling demons that may cause one to be tricked into sickness and death. Depression is one of satan's primary strategies to destroy God's people.

You don't have to fall prey to satan. You can remove the dark cover and open the door to God's presence, and it's so easy to do. Simply open your mouth and begin to talk to God.

> *"For with the heart man believes unto righteousness, and with the mouth confession is made unto salvation."*
> (Romans 10:10 KJV)

Depression is caused by anxiety, and God has instructed us:

> *"Be anxious for nothing, but in everything by prayer and supplication with thanksgiving let your requests be made known to God."*
> (Philippians 4:6 NASB)

Gladness will come to you simply by opening your mouth and speaking God's Word, declaring 'good words' over yourself and your future. Read Proverbs 12:25 again; *"Anxiety in the heart of man causes depression, But a good word makes it glad."* Not only do we talk to God and remind Him of what He has promised us, but we also talk to the devil and command him to take his filthy hands off us and our affairs. Do not yield to any spirits suggesting that you remain quiet. Ask God to forgive you for your sins and ask Jesus to come into your heart, if you have not already done so. Then begin to praise the Lord with your whole heart. As you open your mouth praising God, you bid His presence. God is never going to force entry into your life, but your invitation of praise causes Him to rush before you and get involved in your situation.

> *"But thou art holy, O thou that inhabitest the praises of Israel . . . Rejoice in the LORD, O you righteous! For praise from the upright is beautiful. Praise the LORD with the harp. Make melody to Him with an instrument of ten strings. Sing to Him a new song; Play skillfully with a shout of joy."*
> (Psalm 22:3, 33:1-3 KJV)

When you follow these instructions, the spirit of depression or oppression will flee. satan cannot remain where the Presence of God dwells, and your praises cause God to dwell in your temple (1 Corinthians 3:16).

> *"For thus says the High and Lofty One Who inhabits eternity, whose name is Holy: 'I dwell in the high and holy place, With him who has a contrite and humble spirit, To revive the spirit of the humble, And to revive the heart of the contrite ones.' "*
>
> (Isaiah 57:15 NKJV)

All pride has vanished and humility has taken its place. God is pleased to come in and cause His Joy to overtake you. He revives and restores all those who come to Him with a humble, broken, and contrite spirit.

> *"The sacrifices of God are a broken spirit; a broken and contrite heart, O God, you will not despise."*
>
> (Psalm 51:17 NIV)

> *"[God comes] to console those who mourn in Zion, To give them beauty for ashes, The oil of joy for mourning, The garment of praise for the spirit of heaviness."*
>
> (Isaiah 61:3 NKJV)

When one allows depression to set in, he or she is brought under a curse (Deuteronomy 28:47-48). Depression is an enemy, and it hinders your progress to enjoying 'good success'. Depression cuts off your joy, and God has warned us against its tactics:

> *"Although the fig tree shall not blossom, neither shall fruit be in the vines; the labour of the olive shall fail, and the fields shall yield no meat; the flock shall be cut off from the fold, and there shall be no herd in the stalls: Yet I will rejoice in the LORD, I will joy in the God of*

my salvation. The LORD God is my strength, and he will make my feet like hinds' feet, and he will make me to walk upon mine high places. To the chief singer on my stringed instruments."

(Habakkuk 3:17-19 KJV)

Here, God is saying that no matter what happens, rejoice in Him! Your rejoicing allows Him to do a work in your life, which will propel you to high places. Whenever and wherever you do not find joy, know that the Thief is at work. The devil comes to steal your joy so that he can make a victim of you, but a ceaseless flow of joy will cause your spiritual life to blossom. Deliberately engage yourself in Heaven's bliss and keep yourself from depression.

"The ox knoweth his owner, and the ass his master's crib: but Israel doth not know, my people doth not consider."

(Isaiah 1:3 KJV)

Certainly you are smarter than an ox or a donkey. Begin to read, commit to memory and speak God's Word, and prove that you are smarter than the ox, the donkey, and certainly the devil. When you hear a little voice saying, "I feel sick," or, "I'm a bit weak," proclaim God's Word, which is life! Joel 3:10 says, " . . . *let the weak say I am strong."* Know the Promises of your Master and speak what He tells you to speak. When you speak His Word, you are reinforcing divine nature into your body. When you agree with God's Word, you are showing Him that you know, trust, and depend upon Him, and that you expect Him to release His blessings to you.

Lack of Sleep

When my mother first moved to Florida with me, I was gravely concerned about her health. Generally, when I left home for work at 9:30 in the morning, she was always asleep. This did not cause me concern because I knew many elderly people who enjoyed sleeping as late as ten or eleven in the morning. But weeks passed, and she slept until four or five late in the afternoon. I telephoned my sister about our mother getting too much sleep, and she agreed that this was not a good sign. Out of concern, I began getting up in the wee hours of the morning to check on her, and it did not take me long to realize that my mother was staying up watching TV all night long. After having a serious talk with her and explaining that her sleep patterns played a giant role in her health problems including weight gain, she rebelled, determined to keep late hours. According to her, the shows she enjoyed most did not come on until the wee hours of the morning.

Have you ever heard that your loved ones are the last persons in the world who will listen to you? That was the case with my mother. Here we are, six years later, and a few nights ago she called me into her bedroom to read an article from *Prevention Magazine*, which stated that the lack of proper sleep induces weight gain. "Well, what do you know?" was all I could say.

As I write this story, I wish I could say that I prayed and asked God to send laborers to my mother, informing her of the harm she was doing to her body by staying up late at night. But I didn't; this was one of the needless pains I bore because I did not carry the problem to God in prayer. Thank God for eventually planting information into her hands and giving her an ear with which to hear.

Psychologist and South African instructor, Dr. Laurie Pawlik-Kienlen, informs us that in addition to weight gain unto obesity, lack of sleep also causes depression and low self-esteem. Sleep deprivation or insomnia is also associated with other serious health problems, such as diabetes, cardiovascular diseases, loss of memory, increased appetite through hormonal changes, tremors, clumsiness, and more. According to the National Sleep Foundation, your entire body suffers when you do not get enough good sleep. Your motor functions may become impaired, causing your reaction to be delayed. Never underestimate how important sleep is to your entire life and well-being. See to it that you are getting a good night's rest so that you are mentally, physically, and emotionally healthy.

As a solution, do not do as I did and fail to engage God into your situation when you find that you are unable to sleep. Instead, remind God of His Promise to make your sleep sweet.

"When you lie down, you will not be afraid; when you lie down, your sleep will be sweet."

(Proverbs 3:24 NIV)

Chapter Ten

COME ASIDE AND REST AWHILE

"And He said to them, "Come aside by yourselves to a deserted place and rest a while." For there were many coming and going, and they did not even have time to eat."

(Mark 6:31 NKJV)

The devil is a bold curse. With all of the resources I have available to me, satan still managed to attack my body with a stroke. He is a persistent foe, and although he may disappear, it is only for a season. Before I invite you into the drama, be mindful that Proverbs 26:2 (KJV) says *". . . the curse causeless shall not come."* As bold as satan is, he is completely powerless and cannot operate without an open door. It is the same law of cause and effect: For every action, there is a corresponding effect.

I do not take pride in admitting that I am a bit of a workaholic. I work five and a half days a week, study on Saturday afternoons, and minister every Sunday, not to mention the other significant activities I am actively involved in, especially decreeing Jacksonville, Florida a drug-free city! (I get excited each time I think of the progress we are making.) Activities I consider *significant* are those that God has commissioned me to perform. Not by a long shot do I subscribe to the adage that the people who work the hardest are the ones who get the job done. Also, I do not make these claims boastfully, knowing that even as Jesus instructed His disciples to come aside and rest awhile, He intends for us to operate with wisdom and get ample rest. Our beliefs and choices in life must conform to God's commands and laws, if we are to please Him. When it comes to work, God gave Moses a perfect solution through his wise father-in-law Jethro. Here is my version of the story:

> Jethro watched the diminishing joy of his lonely daughter, Zipporah, and weighed the unreasonable time that Moses was spending counseling and working on behalf of the Israelites. Jethro was disturbed by the neglect his daughter and her family were suffering. Moses was drained, giving Godly counsel to the people from morning to night, and it had taken a toll on him.

> Out of weighty concern, Jethro asked Moses, "Son, look at you, and look at all the people of Israel you are helping. You began before sunrise this morning, and here it is almost sunset. There are still twenty or thirty people in line, waiting to hear a word from the Lord. You haven't stopped today to get a morsel of bread to eat, and when you get home, you are no good for yourself or your devoted wife, who happens to be my daughter. Why don't you get some help?"

> Moses, being the humble man he was, said, "Dad, they trust me. They know me. And, they know that I will not steer them wrong. They want to hear what God is saying, and they know that I have direct contact with Him. I cannot let God's people down, Dad. There are times when our town would be in an uproar if they did not come for advice to help settle their disputes. You know that the Word of God will prick their hearts, and truth always prevails."

> "Yes, son, but what about your wife? And, what about the children?"

Moses dropped his head and whispered, "Yes, sir, my wonderful Zipporah. I love her so much, and I know God is going to permit me to make it up to her. She is such a faithful wife and a wonderful mother to the children she has given me." *Just don't make her angry*, he thought but did not share.

"Son, you are killing yourself, and you are depriving the people of developing, of growing and using their God-given talents. Everything you need is right here for you, but you have overlooked it. God is with you, my son, and because God is with you, His wisdom is also with you, but you haven't asked Him.

"Allow me to teach you. Here is what you should do: First, you have got to teach the people the laws of God, and let them know that God wants them to walk in His laws and His statutes, just as you have purposed in your heart to do. Then, choose from among those who show progress and are holy and faithful, the ones who fear the Almighty God, and teach them to hear God's voice. Choose one to oversee every ten people. Choose one to oversee the five overseers of the ten, then an overseer for the hundreds, the thousands, and so forth. They will judge the people in all seasons for all reasons, and the larger matters they shall bring to you. That way, you will not be burdened, and you will remain in God's Will, giving you even more time to spend with your Lord and valuable time with your family."

And Moses hearkened to the voice of his father-in-law, and he was saved from the stress and burden brought on by the people through satan's deception. And Moses lived 120 years, but still had 20/20 vision, and his natural force was not diminished.[3] Moses had the same strength in old age as he did at thirty.

Here, the man of God was working so hard that he was wearing himself into a frazzle and probably inviting a stroke or heart attack. Although it was an agrarian age and food was at its finest, Moses did not stop to take time and eat properly. But God, in all His infinite mercy, knew the exact laborer to send to His servant, Moses, to get him to change course. Moses was wise, and he listened to his father-in-law.

Remember, Proverbs 26:2 says, "*. . . the curse causeless shall not come.*" This, I can say with confidence: My body talks to me, and so does yours. God also talks to those of us who know His Voice, and He warns us. Warning always comes before destruction. God had warned me to rest, and the signs were not few in number. Warnings of a stroke were certainly there much earlier, but before I go into details, let's talk about the so-called 'silent killer' — the heart attack.

Chapter Eleven

HEART ATTACK:
THE SILENT KILLER?

"In a dream, for instance, a vision at night, when men and women are deep in sleep, fast asleep in their beds— God opens their ears and impresses them with warnings To turn them back from something bad they're planning, from some reckless choice, And keep them from an early grave, from the river of no return."

(Job 33:15 MSG)

"Then Peter opened his mouth, and said, Of a truth I perceive that God is no respecter of persons: But in every nation he that feareth him, and worketh righteousness, is accepted with him."

(Acts 10:34-35 KJV)

This, of course, is one of God's provisional Promises. God will never do more for one of His children than He does for another, because He is no respecter of persons, but He does regard those who fear Him and work righteousness. When we remain under His protective care, God sometimes overlooks our foolish conduct, overrides our careless mistakes, and showers us with His endless Mercy. I believe this is what He means when He had the psalmist David write that He understands that our frail frames are made of dust, and that is why He has mercy on us.

"As a father pities his children, So the LORD pities those who fear Him. For He knows our frame; He remembers that we are dust. As for man, his days are like grass; As a flower of the field, so he flourishes. For the wind passes over it, and it is gone, And its place remembers it no more. But the mercy of the LORD is from everlasting to everlasting On those who fear Him, And His righteousness to children's children, To such as keep His covenant, And to those who remember His commandments to do them."

(Psalm 103:13-18 NKJV)

For some in the medical and related fields, to characterize a heart attack as a 'silent killer' is an outright blatant deception and one of satan's oldest tricks. This undeniable fact is clearly established by the American Physiological Society.

To characterize a Heart Attack as a 'silent killer' is outright blatant deception.
The devil wants you to ignore the symptoms.

God, with His masterful creativity, made two genders: male and female. While there are some gender-based variations in advanced warnings of heart attacks, greater are the similarities. And, in both cases, the bottom line is, there are definitely warnings. This completely wipes out the 'silent killer' theory. Study after study has been conducted, and the most credible conclusions concur with the advanced study published by the American Physiological Society:

"Sexual Dimorphism in the Presentation of Cardiovascular Disease — We are all taught that there are three hallmarks of a heart attack: Chest

discomfort or uncomfortable pressure, fullness, squeezing, or pain in the center of the chest that lasts longer than a few minutes or that comes and goes and spreads pain to one or both arms, back, jaw, or stomach. Cold sweats and nausea.

It turns out that these three hallmarks are experienced more often by men than by women, and, in fact only one in three women have these symptoms when experiencing a myocardial infarction. Instead, women experience shortness of breath, nausea, vomiting, sleeplessness, back or jaw pain, and/or a feeling of generalized fatigue or weakness, weeks prior to an acute myocardial infarction! The serious consequence is that appropriate treatment for women is delayed, inappropriate, or incorrect, leading to preventable deaths. Current studies of disease processes and diagnostic procedures are demonstrating that there is a need not only to recognize that differences exist between men and women, but also to perform appropriate studies documenting normal and pathophysiological parameters, especially as they relate to diagnostic procedures. Studies of this nature are leading to the evaluation of diagnostic modalities, such as exercise ECGs and cardiac-imaging modalities, with respect to sex differences to improve the diagnosis and risk assessment of women and men, specifically, with suspected cardiovascular disease." (Advanced Physiology Education, 31:17-22, 2007; Internet, www.psysiology.org)

The term 'silent killer' is just another way the devil tricks us into sickness. Because we hear the expression coming from the mouth of a professional with an MD or some other earned academic title following his name, without questioning the validity of the finding, without asking to see conclusive research, without protecting our lives, we accept the phrase as truth. So, because the doctor says that heart attacks are silent killers, it must be 'silent' — Baloney!

Since we are on the subject of medical doctors, please know that despite any less-than-positive statements I may make about doctors, I believe in all that Jesus believes in. Because Dr. Luke was a part of His inner circle, it seems clear to me that we most definitely need doctors. In Dr. Luke's day, the primary source for treating patients was herbs. Remember, also, that he was a follower of Christ. As you research to establish the credibility of your doctor, I believe you should check to see if your prospect has Jesus in his or her life. One of the very first questions you should ask is, "Are you saved?"

I remember when a friend of mine here in Jacksonville accompanied me to an ophthalmologist, out of my mother's and her concern about the blepharospasms attacking my eyes. The kind doctor entered the room, introduced himself, placed his seeing eye tab on his head, pulled up a rolling stool, and beckoned me to come close.

I pulled back. "Doctor, are you saved?"

The doctor was dumbfounded. He knew what I was asking, but he could not believe the question and responded, "Pardon?"

"I asked, are you saved? Have you received Jesus Christ as your Lord and Savior?"

"Y-y-e-s-s-s?" He stumbled through the three letter word and ended with a question as if to say, 'Are you comfortable with that?'

"You *are* saved, then?"

"Oh, yes," he responded, this time with confidence.

"All right, then you may look at my eyes."

Ladies and gentlemen, let's get our priorities in order. The first thing the receptionist wants to know when I enter the doctor's office is how I'm going to pay. I wonder what would happen if I said that I could *not* pay; however, since I can, the doctor's fees must be ascertained before I can proceed with treatment. This means that I am retaining a service or hiring the doctor to work for me. This is the way it goes: I hire you and you provide a service. I pay you the fee that you quote to me. You earn a living.

I have heard so many horror stories of how doctors treat patients, and the patients, rather than firing the doctor, will endure the pain, and some will even keep going to the disrespectful doctor. I can almost assure you that any discourteous, unempathizing, unsympathetic doctor is not a born-again Christian. After all, you can tell the tree by the fruit it bears.

> *"Even so every good tree bringeth forth good fruit; but a corrupt tree bringeth forth evil fruit."*
> (Matthew 7:17 KJV)

The fruits of the born-again spirit are love, joy, patience, longsuffering, kindness, gentleness, and so on (Galatians 5:22-23). What does light have to do with darkness (2 Corinthians 6:14)? How can two walk together except they are in agreement (Amos 3:3)?

Listen to me closely: When it comes to your health, always be guarded. Learn all you can about someone who is earning a living based on your infirmity. When a physician has treated you for an illness for more than a few weeks (Generally, one can tell the difference in a matter of days.), and you are not improving in your health, something is wrong. You should feel as wonderful at sixty or seventy as you did at thirty or forty, or even at a hundred and twenty, because Moses did, and God is no respecter of persons.

I cannot warn you enough, as Dr. Whitaker admonished us years back: Do not place your life in the hands of a medical doctor. It doesn't mean, 'Do not go to the doctor', but that you are to take charge of your own life. Read, study, and ask questions. This is the information age, and anything you are concerned about can be researched over the Internet. Simply because the doctor has you on medications doesn't mean you should remain on those medications until they kill you. This is exactly what millions are doing. According to one major magazine, an early report revealed that doctors own 80% of all stocks in the pharmaceutical industry. Why wouldn't they prescribe medications to you so freely?

Back when the doctors gave my dad five days to live because medications had weakened his heart so dramatically, I took action. My dad lived in Indiana; my sister was there helping my physically exhausted mother, who swore Daddy was also suffering from Alzheimer's. Unbeknownst to Mother, after I had researched his meds, I had my sister discontinue a certain medication, and, unsurprisingly, my dad's memory was restored immediately. Another sister here in Florida had more liberty than I, so we agreed that she would go home to help my sister and follow my instructions in taking Daddy off some of the other deadly high blood pressure medications. At the time, his legs had swollen and he had fluid building up around his heart. It never fails: Over a period of time, beta-blockers, along with Lasix, will cause fluid buildup and gradually give you congestive heart failure. Read the warnings; the symptoms are almost always the same.

Nutritional supplements were quickly rising to lead alternative healing in the mainstream. We changed Daddy's diet and gave him high doses of CoQ10 in the purest form (which also helps to prevent fluid buildup), 1200mg of magnesium daily (Doctors who practice nutritional healing say this heals the inner heart, among many other valuable contributions.), Whole Food Multi-Vitamin, and pure fish oil.

We also administered super green foods, which was an absolute no-no for doctors because green foods consist of vitamin K, which helps the blood coagulate. However, in addition to the CoQ10, we also gave Daddy high doses of vitamin E, mixed tocopherol, and plenty of garlic, all of which help to keep the blood flowing. Mind you, according to the nation's top nutritionists and medical doctors who practice alternative healing, super green foods are an absolute yes-yes.

Ezekiel 47:12 says, "... and the fruit thereof shall be for meat, and the leaf thereof for medicine." These were not synthetics made of tar and plastics, which the body could not possibly absorb; rather, they were foods grown in the soil, the good earth from which the body was created. We used God's very simple prescription, the leaves for medicine, and my dad lived eight years longer as a result. When Daddy did pass over, it was because of the damage the medications had caused to his kidneys. In all honesty, I believe we could have rebuilt Dad's kidneys through prayer and nutrients, but because of the distance, I had little control over my mother placing him on dialysis. God says His Word is health to all our flesh, including the kidneys. We must, however, apply His laws.

There is a light at the end of the tunnel. Many physicians today are listening to patients who enjoy good health, and they have begun prescribing nutritional supplements. Mass media has introduced doctors such as Dr. Oz, who has stood his ground when challenging some of the die-hard gougers. Thank God, too, for those people who have read, studied, sought professional advice, built up their systems, changed their dietary practices, and then completely taken themselves off medications. They go to the doctor for a checkup, but when it comes to treatments, they come to the health food store. Ten years later, we are enjoying the fulfillment of God's Word, where He promises that knowledge shall increase (Daniel 12:4).

The only inerrant truth is God's Word. Fear and intimidation often cause us to become trapped in bondage and tricked into sickness. The Bible clearly teaches us to TRUST NO MAN.

"Woe to them that go down to Egypt for help; and stay on horses, and trust in chariots, because they are many; and in horsemen, because they are strong, but they look not unto the Holy One of Israel, neither seek the LORD!"
(Isaiah 31:1 KJV)

"Put not your trust in princes, nor in the son of man, in whom there is no help."
(Psalm 146:3 KJV)

"Blessed is that man that maketh the LORD his trust, and respected not the proud, nor such as turn aside to lies."
(Psalm 40:4 KJV)

"Lo, this is the man that made not God his strength, but trusted in the abundance of his riches, And strengthened himself in his wickedness."
(Psalm 52:7 ASV)

"In God have I put my trust: I will not be afraid what man can do unto me."
(Psalm 56:11 KJV)

"And in the thirty-ninth year of his reign, Asa became diseased in his feet, and his malady was severe; yet in his disease he did not seek the LORD, but the physicians. So Asa rested with his fathers; he died in the forty-first year of his reign."
(2 Chronicles 16:12-13 NKJV)

King Asa died because he did not mix the Lord with the doctor. God will always send warning signals to us that something is off track through the mechanical makeup of this marvelous, machine-like body that He has designed for us. The devil comes along and tells us the body gives us no warning signals and to ignore such sensations as meaningless. I've even heard it said, "Everybody gets a little pain in the head from time to time." How absurd! Pain is a curse, and for every curse, there is a cause.

The day has come for all God's children to take His Word seriously. Faith is a way of life, and that way includes applying His principles to your health. The true Christian life lines up totally with the Word of God, which only says what God says. Only when God confirms a report do we honor the report. Otherwise, God's Word is our final authority.

ONLY WHEN GOD CONFIRMS A REPORT DO WE HONOR THE REPORT

We are not ignorant of satan's devices. Don't waste your time on useless busywork, the barren pursuits of darkness. Expose these things for the sham they are. It's a scandal when people waste their lives on things they must do in the darkness where no one will see. Rip the cover off frauds and see how unattractive they look in the light of Christ. Wake up from your sleep. Climb out of your coffins. Christ will show you the light! Watch your step and use your head, but make the most of every chance you get. These are desperate times. (Ephesians 5:11-16 The Message)

God has instructed us to expose the devil and reveal the truth whenever and wherever we find deception reigning. The 'silent killer' error ends today, with you! You are now enlightened. It is your responsibility to share that there is no such thing as a "silent killer" with all whom you come in contact. The propaganda is another one of satan's too-long-lived tricks, encouraging the masses to ignore the signs of a heart attack building up in the body, when the body is letting them know that something is going wrong. Small signs may develop in your body. For example, you may suddenly begin to have sleepless nights. Pay attention, eat plenty of celery, and go to the doctor for an examination! Or, you may develop nausea, vomit for no established reason, or just feel sick. Stop and get checked out; remember that these are serious warnings, not silent. Small warnings, such as nausea or sleeplessness, may seem like minor displeasures, but they are God's alarm signals, innately woven into your DNA. They may be rated as minor, annoying irritations or displeasures, but, nonetheless, these are signs.

The term 'silent killer' was coined by Dr. Gerald Reaven in his book, *X-Syndrome*. I applaud him for the simplicity and clarity of his writing, making it easy for a layman such as I to comprehend. However, God said that the curse causeless shall not come, which implies that there will be some sort of indication or warning and a counteraction one can apply to one's body or lifestyle to avert or circumvent a curse. God has designed the body so brilliantly that if monitored, we will detect signals when something is out of order.

> *"For there is nothing covered, that shall not be revealed; neither hid, that shall not be known."*
>
> (Luke 12:2 KJV)

God is not the kind of Father who would design a temple or dwelling place in which He desires to reside but makes no provision for you to perform maintenance and keep it up. Moreover, God has promised, *"The Lord will perfect that which concerneth me: thy mercy, O Lord, endureth for ever: forsake not the works of thine own hands,"* (Psalm 138:8 KJV). There are three extremely significant Promises in this Scripture:

1) The Lord will make every situation in my life wonderful. In addition, He will cause any troubling thing or situation to benefit me.

2) The Lord's Mercy is infinite, and He views me only through His eyes of love and kindness.

3) Because God is our Maker, He will not forsake that which He has formed and created.

God has created automatic control systems in the body, and these systems signal the body to go, yield, and stop. The 'go' sign indicates that the body is properly fueled and maintained with vegetables, fruit, protein, vitamins, minerals, water, exercise, rest, and fresh air. The 'yield' or 'caution' signs come when the body feels pretty good most of the time, but there are infrequent headaches, or days when a pain strikes here or there, or some nights are restless, or you can't hold anything in your stomach, or you are just plain tired all the time. These uncomfortable annoyances are irritating but not so inconvenient that we must interrupt our daily affairs. One's world doesn't have to stop when the warning comes, but one must remember to operate in wisdom, because these signs are not to be taken for granted.

While you are waiting for the results of your medical examination, stop eating red meats, sugar, white bread, white rice, and processed junk foods. If these items are permanently eliminated from your diet, you'll be amazed at how much better your body functions. Making minor adjustments makes a tremendous difference. It's so easy to ignore or overlook the warning signs your body emits, but decide in your heart that from this moment forward you will be more responsible. We must never forget that your body is the temple of the Holy Spirit, and neglecting the body grieves Him.

I can never forget a story I heard many years ago: A group of tourists visited Spain, which has a great reputation for its ancient historical sites, and they were determined to view at least one of its magnificent monasteries. One in particular was located upon the side of the cliff and was so beautiful, but the only way to reach it was for some of the monks to pull you up in a basket. The ride in the basket up to the cliff was thrilling, and the tour was more than the group had expected, but afterward they had to return to the basket to get back down.

It was easier for them to look up than to look down, only now, realizing the height they had climbed. "Wow," they said, "we've got a long distance to go." Now, they paid closer attention to how they were going to be lowered, and they all examined the basket. The rope holding the basket was badly raveled and threads sprouted out. Gravely concerned when they saw the danger they were in, they asked the monk in charge, "How often do you change this rope, sir?"

The monk was quick to reply, "Why, we change it every time it breaks, of course."

It is also my prayer, as one of the main purposes of this book, that you do not ignore the slightest uncomfortable sign your body relays to you. Get professional help at the first sign of irregularities, provided you are not spiritually *and* professionally equipped to administer healing remedies to yourself.

You may ask, "Have you ever had a heart attack? How do you know how one feels?" Yes, I have had a heart attack. By now you have figured out that I certainly have not acted in the most responsible ways when it comes to my own health. This is another reason I can attest to the wonderful mercies of God.

Five years ago, the Lord began to nudge me to take a rest. The urge was there so strongly, but I grieved the Holy Spirit by ignoring Him. Finally, one by one, God began sending His servants and handmaidens into the shop to advise me to take a rest vacation. As far as I can count, there were seven different ministers and prophets. One of the prophets specifically informed me that God had sent him all the way from Wisconsin just to tell me to take a three-week vacation. Long distant, indeed, because I was in Florida. Did I obey? Nope — too busy.

Then, one day, as I was walking into the shop office, crossing almost the same spot where I was standing when I was attacked by a stroke, the most excruciating pain pierced my heart. It felt like a dagger was being jabbed through its very tip. The pain was sharper than the deadliest blade, quicker than a flash of lightening, and tinier than the point of a pin. Before I could say or think anything, it was gone. The pain left as suddenly as it had come; the attack was over in a split second, and I felt fine. No, I felt great. I stood in the doorway of my office and placed my hand over my heart. "Oooow," I whispered, "that was a heart attack," I analyzed what had just happened, measuring the pain that had attacked the base of my heart, which covered a spot no more than the size of the tip of a pin.

Boy, did I begin praising and thanking God for protecting me. I thanked Him that my body was so nutritionally strong that it had withstood any damage the attack had planned to cause and for rescuing me from the snares of satan's clutches. The seven people who God sent as messengers were not a watch but a warning, and I was at least wise enough to know that this was a more severe warning than the messengers. I closed down the shop, went home, and rested for a few days. Those days were greatly refreshing, spent in the presence of the Lord.

God had instructed and even warned me to stop and rest, just as He instructed His disciples.[4] I can just imagine how the disciples felt when He told them to take a break. Oh, to have been there to hear the Lord teach the Word to His chosen ones. The disciples could not resist sharing:

> ". . . Did not our heart burn within us, while he talked with us by the way, and while he opened to us the scriptures?"
>
> (Luke 24:32 KJV)

Rest was the farthest thing from their minds, for it was exciting to watch Jesus heal the sick, cast out demons, and even raise the dead. The anointing permeated the air, and they enjoyed a constant, invigorating lift. It's difficult to come down when you are experiencing the awesomeness of God's Presence at each waking hour. Those men thought they could go forever without rest. After all, they were living in the very Presence of the Messiah.

But, Jesus, knowing that the body is man's contact with the natural realm, understood that theirs were weakening day by day. The Apostle Paul writes, *"For which cause we faint not; but though our outward man perish, yet the inward man is renewed day by day."* (2 Corinthians 4:16 KJV) Thus, the body could not be sustained without rest. Therefore, He ordered His disciples to stop and rest (see Mark 6:31).

More than anything in this world, I love being in the Presence of the Lord. There is no greater joy than experiencing God's tangible anointing or supping at the Father's Feet and have the Holy Spirit illuminate the Word of God to me. When the Holy Spirit imparts revelation of God's Word, the closest thing I can compare it to is like taking a ride through Heaven on the wings of wind. Nothing compares.

Next to being with my Lord, I am fascinated when I am able to minister to others. Working in the public sphere, with no political restrictions being dictated to me about exercising my faith, allows me the opportunity to minister healing, salvation, and deliverance on a daily basis. When a lost soul comes to the Lord, it's as though I have just been injected with a premium shot of Glory. I stay on a Holy High. As a result, it seems that I never tire, but 'seems' is appropriate, because there are consequences to overtaxing the body, even though it will endeavor to dictate to you.

We must remember, *"It is the spirit that quickened, the flesh profited nothing . . ."* (John 6:63 NKJV). I am even more aware of how much more powerful the mind is over the body. Again, John Milton wrote in 1667, "The mind is its own place and commands a heaven of hell or a hell of heaven." Understand that the body is the weakest part of the triune man and therefore requires the most care and attention.

Chapter Twelve

THE STROKE ATTACK

"He sent His word and healed them, And delivered them from their destructions."

(Psalm 107:20 NASB)

This particular afternoon, I was walking through the office when I felt the right side of my back begin to contort. Fortunately, I didn't have to deal with any customers in the store. Right away I recognized that I was being attacked with a stroke. Notice that I use the word 'attack', because as far as I'm concerned, the enemy was demonstrating an act of aggression in an attempt to afflict my body. An attack is all that it was.

Now it was up to me to counter the attack. I never permitted the word 'stroke' to pass my lips. Oh, I knew what it was, but I had only one choice and that was to gird up my loins with the Truth of God's Word. War had ensued, and it was time to get violent. My right arm was being pulled inside my body, and it felt as though it was being bolted into my back. With every ounce of strength I could muster, I pushed my arm out, and at the same time I yelled, *"I POUR THE BLOOD OF JESUS THROUGH MY ARM AND BODY, AND I COMMAND YOU SPIRIT OF STROKE TO GO, IN THE NAME OF JESUS!"* I repeated these words out loud, over and over again, *"LOOSE, YOU INVADING DEMON, GO NOW, IN THE NAME OF JESUS!"*

It was a tug of war! I did not relent, and that demon did not want to, but it had no alternative. The Blood of Jesus is our line of attack and sure defense in all situations. When we plead the Blood of Jesus, sickness and disease must flee.

"And they overcame him by the blood of the Lamb, and by the word of their testimony; and they loved not their lives unto death."

(Revelation 12:11 KJV)

The war lasted about five minutes, until the demon finally conceded. What else could it do but bow to the Name of Jesus? Philippians 2:10 (KJV) promises, *"That at the name of Jesus every knee should bow, of things in heaven, and things in earth, and things under the earth . . ."* The word 'Every' includes stroke-demons.

I fully knew my rights as a committed, uncompromising Christian and executed them. I had not waited until this intrusive attack occurred to plead the protective Blood of Jesus. I make it a daily practice to honor and thank God for giving me His precious Son who shed His Blood at Calvary for my salvation. I often remind Him that salvation covers every act of deliverance for my life. I was rooted and grounded in my foundation of faith, and God honored His Word. I practice God's Presence on an on-going basis, and because I dwell in the shadow of the Almighty, I was able to receive the Promise that no danger or evil shall come nigh my dwelling places — my body, home, and workplace.

I grabbed my keys and bag, closed up the shop, and left work, feeling the aftereffects of the battle. My right shoulder and armpit were in obscured pain, and I had little mobility in the lower portion of my right arm. The pain was there, but I suppose my adrenaline was racing so high that I did not realize it. The only thing I could think of was, "Get someone to pray with you." I needed all the prayer I could get, so I drove about two miles to the home of my friend, Prophet Brian Carn. Wouldn't you know it, he wasn't there, but a guest who answered the door was kind enough to pray with me right there in the doorway.

After thanking her, I hurried back to my car and drove another three miles to my home. I couldn't wait to get from the garage to my bed. I remember dropping my bag and keys on the sofa and plunking down on the bed, clothes and all. No doubt the adrenaline was slowing down, because pain was now wreaking havoc in my shoulder. The instant I lay down, indescribable pain resurfaced. I placed my hand on the pain. As a rule, when praying for others in pain, I simply say something like, "Pain, *go!*" But that was not my prayer for myself. Instead, I said, "Lord, I'm Your child, and You know how faithfully I serve You . . . I'm not supposed to hurt like this." I don't know the point at which God responded during those five seconds when I was putting Him in remembrance of my covenant with Him and reasoning with Him. But I do know that before those words were finished, the pain was gone. My shoulder felt better than ever, and no pain has returned since.

The next day, I was back at work because I had no one to run the shop. I felt really great, but when I attempted to use the computer, I realized that much of the mobility in my right hand had gone. "Oh, no, you don't," I threatened that demon of infirmity, "Not here." My words were soft-spoken, but my spirit was screaming with anger. I could lift, pull, push, and so forth, but it was a challenge to use the computer. This lasted for two days. I relentlessly continued pouring the Blood of Jesus through my arm and speaking wholeness, in addition to exercising my hand. On the third day, as quickly as the limp arm had occurred, mobility was restored, and I have been whole from that day to this one.

Thank God for my mother. I often accuse her of revealing too much about my affairs, but this was one time I was glad when she telephoned my sister and told her of the attack, because my sister came to the rescue. She was so dear that she brought my nephew to Florida with her, and the two of them spent two or three weeks working at the store while I took a vacation. My nephew stayed even longer and worked alongside me for another few weeks. Did I ever enjoy the time away . . . and then together with Him, too!

There is nothing that goes wrong in your body that isn't preceded by a signal, cuing you in on an impending disaster. Long before having the stroke attack, I had many signals. Days and even weeks before, I had mentioned to my mother that I was experiencing headaches. I never have headaches. Those were warning signs. I had been very slack in taking proper nutrients, especially vitamin E, though for what reason I cannot say. I can only say that I was not consistent with my regime. I had also stopped exercising.

The Holy Spirit nudged me countless times to shut down the store and rest, but I did not. Instead, I took energy pills with stimulants almost on a daily basis. I would wake up each morning, practically listless, but after brushing my teeth and taking a shower, I prepared a little mixture of the stimulant pill with various antioxidants to counter the effects of the free radicals. That was a huge problem. Any ingredient promoting superficial energy is dangerous, and I know this better than anyone, but I rejected the knowledge. I was tricked into thinking that the stimulants were working for me when all along they were working against me.

I know satan would enjoy seeing me out of his way, if for no other reason than the reality that I am such a bold saint. I have no problem calling a sin a sin, and wherever it rears its ugly head, I expose it. But out of deception, I refused to stop and rest. Instead, I sought an alternative, knowing there is none. *"For sin, taking occasion by the commandment, deceived me, and by it slew me,"* (Romans 7:11 KJV). Dishonoring my body caused the stroke attack; the stroke attack was the curse. Thank God that even when we are in error He does not withhold His promises from us. Through our many sins, His hand is not turned away and He continues to stretch his hand toward us. Weapons may form against us, but they cannot prosper.

The key is knowledge. God said His people perish or die because they do not know who they are or what they have been given through His Son's death, burial, and resurrection. How often do we hear Christians quoting Scripture after Scripture yet living a life of defeat and emptiness? Too many Christians have what I call 'head knowledge', which gives you intellect, not true knowledge; God chooses foolish things of this world to confound or put to shame man's intellect.

> *"But God hath chosen the foolish things of the world to confound the wise; and God hath chosen the weak things of the world to confound the things which are mighty."*
> (1 Corinthians 1:27 KJV)

To successfully enjoy a life of Heaven on Earth, or to successfully triumph in both the natural and spirit realms, just knowing God's Word is not enough. Just knowing God's Word and not appropriating it is having a form of godliness but denying the power thereof. Doctrine is mere words on paper; too many churches preach doctrine and even have bitter feuds over it. Shame, shame. God's Word does not become life until doctrine comes from the pages into the activities of your everyday life. The blind see, the lame walk, deaf ears are opened, and the dead are raised. That's the Spirit of God's Word brought to life. The letter kills, but the Spirit gives Life. When Jesus is involved, His Word is Spirit and it brings Life!

Fall in love with God. Spend time with Him by feasting on His Word. Tell Him over and over how much you love Him. You will be so surprised at some of His responses. As He did me, He may even respond by telling you that He loves you, too. God is looking for 'heart knowledge'. When we understand our righteous position with God through the Blood-bought Covenant — the price Christ Jesus paid for us to enjoy our position in God's family — when we take God's Word seriously by obeying God's commands, being doers of the Word and not hearers only, when we claim God's healing Promises for our very own, and when we apply the Blood of Jesus to any infirmity introduced into our bodies, then we will witness that the Messiah is Jehovah Rapha, the God who heals!

Attack: Sickness or Symptom?

If you do not remember all I share with you, just remember this and act accordingly: A physical attack of infirmity is not a sickness. An attack is a sharp blow waiting to become embedded in your spirit at the time of its assault. Sickness, on the other hand, is an existing condition or illness.

A PHYSICAL ATTACK OF INFIRMITY IS NOT A SICKNESS.

The attack does not become sickness until you have spoken it, claimed it, and failed to usurp its authority over you by applying the Word of God and the Blood of the Lamb. Revelation 12:11 tells us that when we plead the Blood of Jesus and proclaim our deliverance in the face of adversity, we are conquerors. A satanic attack of infirmity from the devil is a symptom beginning the formation of a sickness, but God has promised that no weapon formed against you shall prosper. (see Isaiah 54:17)

Picture an architect drawing a blueprint of a building. Once he forms the shapes and sizes of the foundation, plumbing, frame, roof, floors, walls, electrical wiring, and so on, the building structure is formed. But this is only a blueprint, a drawing on a piece of paper, until physical, tangible materials begin to construct the edifice. It does not become a literal building until the bricks and mortar have been put in place.

When satan attacks you, if you counter the attack at the onslaught, you will prevail. Timing is everything! Your initial response will determine the outcome. If you accept the blow as a part of your body's activity, that real spirit of infirmity will acknowledge your invitation and become a sickness in your body. How often have you heard someone say, "I'm catching a cold"? The minute the symptom strikes, they claim the disease, and it's only a matter of hours or days before the cold has manifested itself. How unfortunate. Think of the many times a person will claim an illness simply because a member of his or her family has been afflicted. The world calls it a genetic or hereditary illness. Saints of God call it a curse. At the first thought of an illness, begin to fight back with God's Word against the very thought. If the symptom arises, be forceful with the Word of God. More than ever, this is when you must cast down imaginations and pull in God's living Word (2 Corinthians 10:5). With every breath in you, resist the devil and he will flee. (James 4:7)

Suppose I Have a Sickness Now?

If you have not followed these principles and have allowed sickness to linger in your body, simply repent and begin to enjoy your healing. Never accept a sickness in your body, no matter how long it has lingered and no matter who says it cannot be healed. Those are little whispers from satan, a liar, and the only thing a liar does is lie. All tricksters are liars.

> *"What if some did not believe and were without faith? Does their lack of faith and their faithlessness nullify and make ineffective and void the faithfulness of God and His fidelity [to His Word]? By no means! Let God be found true though every human being is false and a liar, as it is written, That You may be justified and shown to be upright in what You say, and prevail when You are judged [by sinful men]."*
>
> (Romans 4:3-4 AMP)

The reason God gives us countless illustrations of His endless Grace in the Bible is to teach us what we can do through Christ Jesus. Certainly if He can create an entire world, He is able to cause limbs to grow. In John 5, the Apostle tells the story of Jesus' return to Jerusalem from a mission trip to celebrate a Jewish holiday. On His way to the temple, He stopped at the pool of Bethesda, which had five covered porches where crowds of sick people lay on the porches, waiting to get into the pool and be healed.

> *"For an angel went down at a certain time into the pool and stirred up the water; then whoever stepped in first, after the stirring of the water, was made well of whatever disease he had. Now a certain man was there who had an infirmity thirty-eight years. When Jesus saw him lying there, and knew that he already had been in that condition a long time, He said to him, 'Do you want to be made well?' The sick man answered Him, 'Sir, I have no man to put me into the pool when the water is stirred up; but while I am coming, another steps down before me.' Jesus said to him, 'Rise, take up your bed and walk.' And immediately the man was made well, took up his bed, and walked."*
>
> (John 5:4-9 NKJV)

There are wonderful saints of God who have had the misfortune of being in an accident and incurring unthinkable injuries, such as paralysis or leg amputations. Some have been struck with an illness and are unable to recover. These great men and women of God have used their disabilities as a tool of encouragement, working daily and proving to the world that life does not have to stop simply because a limb has been amputated or the upper torso doesn't move as it does for most folks.

Two blind men followed Jesus after He had healed the woman with the twelve-year hemorrhaging and caused the little dead girl to rise up. Of healing their blindness, he asked, *"Believe ye that I am able to do this?"* (Matthew 9:28 KJV). They responded in the affirmative, seeing the miracles that He had just worked. Then Jesus touched their eyes and said, *"According to your faith be it unto you,"* and the Bible says that their eyes were opened (see Matthew 9:18-25). As much as you are able to receive from God, He is willing to do for you.

Encouraging others through one's infirmity is so wonderful. But, according to His Word, God is waiting for those individuals who are infirm to simply trust Him to make them whole. Notice again in John 5:6 (NKJV) where Jesus asked, *"Do you want to be made well?"* Not one single Word of God (in the Bible) is void of Power. Here, Jesus is letting the lame know that they have a choice. They could choose to remain infirm, or they could trust Him and receive healing. In every situation, we have a choice. To look to one's circumstance is vain; to look to the Master is victory.

Stay alert! Stay away from doubters. The chief demon satan will send people who will attempt to make you feel ashamed because you are trusting God rather than trusting the doctor. Not many Christians are on the level that God desires them to ascend to when it comes to healing, because they have not developed to spiritual maturation. Demons of sickness are real, and Christians had better begin practicing healing on an on-going basis. Fear is the antithesis of faith. To think that you have to die with some sort of sickness or disease is fear at its final and finest dress rehearsal.

TO THINK THAT YOU MUST DIE WITH A SICKNESS OR DISEASE IS FEAR AT ITS FINEST AND FINAL DRESS REHEARSAL.

Eat healthily, exercise, take your daily nutritional supplements, and above all, clean up your mind by meditating on God's Word day and night. Charles Capps, one of today's

Gospel giants, refers to the Gospel as 'God's pill'. So, take your dose of the Gospel at least daily.

> *"This book of the Law shall not depart from your mouth,*
> *but you shall meditate in it day and night, that you may*
> *observe to do according to all that is written in it. For*
> *then you will make your way prosperous, and then you*
> *will have good success."*
>
> (Joshua 1:8 NKJV)

> *"Be ye doers of the word, and not hearers only, deceiving*
> *your own selves."*
>
> (James 1:22 KJV)

Those who listen to God's Word and refuse to obey are behaving as servants of satan and are being deceived. Benefits come through obedience, and when we are obedient hearers, we position ourselves to walk in divine health. Remember, I did not say, "Do not go to the doctor." Bear in mind that I have worked with nutrients and health issues on a daily basis for over twenty years, which gives me an advantage in self-diagnosis and treatment. I realize that few people are at a level to self-diagnose and treat their own physical condition. This means that you should not hesitate to see a doctor. It's always good to get a checkup.

Chapter Thirteen

LOVE

". . . and the greatest of these is charity."
(1 Corinthians 13:13 KJV)

Y ou haven't enjoyed the power of true Christianity until you've experience the power of love re-routing satan's interference in your affairs. Love gives and heals.

Love Gives

"Blessed art thou, O LORD: teach me thy statutes."
(Psalm 119:12 KJV)

"Open thou mine eyes, that I may behold wondrous things out of thy law."
(Psalm 119:18 KJV)

Reading the Holy Bible for enjoyment is one thing, but following these Words ushers us into an entirely new realm of spiritual understanding. When one or both of these Scriptures are prayed back to God, He opens His Word up to us like the rolling back of heavenly clouds, permitting the radiance of the sun to shine through. I've heard it said that God will give us a revelation of His Word to the degree that we are able to receive it. There is much relevance in this perception; simply ask and it shall be given to you.

I'm learning, however, that God also gives us revelation according to the Plan He has for our lives:

"For I know the thought that I think toward you, saith the Lord, thoughts of peace, and not of evil, to give you an expected end."

(Jeremiah 29:11 KJV)

When God has an assignment for one of His children, He goes to the fullest length to help that child understand what the outcome of that plan will be. Admittedly, at least in my case, God has never given me the details of how to fulfill a mission. He simply ordains the end. When God ordains the end, the means have already been met. We only need to follow through fearlessly and fervently.

First Corinthian 13 is the chapter most of us refer to as the *love* chapter. Oftentimes, when I'm ministering, I remind the audience that love sees no evil. Love is longsuffering, refuses to slander, and is kind at all times, even when others are not in our presence. Love doesn't backbite and is not a hypocrite. Love will never hurt others mentally or otherwise. Love does all in its power to protect and enhance, not to pull down and destroy. I pray to God that these words do not fall on deaf ears.

The facet of love that was recently revealed to me by the Holy Spirit brought such a revelation that I was overtaken with joy. 'So near, yet so far' is an adage we once used frequently. I read the King James Version of the 'love chapter', which addresses 'love' as 'charity'. All my life I have, in some ways, been associated with charitable organizations. I have volunteered for them, supported them financially, referred others to them, and even incorporated my own charitable organization called Success Builders Incorporated.

What I am about to say may seem elementary to many of you, but even though I had read 1 Corinthians 13 countless times before, this reading brought me an explosive revelation.

"Though I speak with the tongues of men and of angels, and have not charity, I am become as a sounding brass, or a tinkling cymbal . . ."

(1 Corinthians 13:1 KJV)

Charity is goodwill, benevolence, and generosity. It means to aid through gifts, contributions, donations, assistance, and offerings. It means compassion and understanding. In other words, charity is giving, giving, giving. When the true meaning of love hit me, I began to reflect upon the many organizations with which I had been or still am affiliated, and I recalled that they were or still are all charitable organizations. All of these organizations were formed to help others; some fed the hungry, some offered legal services, some provided education, and others provided training or jobs. But no matter the byline of the organization, the common thread has always been to somehow help or give, and by law they are all labeled 'charitable' organizations.

Strong's Concordance defines 'charity' as love, so you see, love is helping and giving. To a degree, I knew that 1 Corinthians 13 meant giving, for this is what I have taught others. But to be perfectly honest with you, the power behind the word 'giving' was revealed to me only recently. Love works hard to give!

LOVE WORKS HARD TO GIVE.

Growing up as a young woman, my parents never explained to me the true role of a wife. I had two of the most loving parents a teenager could hope for, but because they did not understand the significance of God's Word, I was never taught the true meaning of love. I was young, attractive, and intelligent; the world taught me that I already had all I needed to make a husband happy. How deceived I was, and how deceived too many young women are today! It took lots of bumps and two divorces before I was born again, and through the teaching of God's Word, I learned the true meaning of love. In fact, I learned the true meaning of life in its entirety.

Because I was left to the wolves in my younger years, I deliberately minister to as many young women as I am able, imparting the true meaning of love. How precious a marriage is when women learn to respect their men, to not look to them for lavish gifts but to build a home as Proverbs 31 says. We must learn that we are there to help, not lead. Dutiful respect shifts the mind toward giving rather than receiving. Respect from men to women is also a must. This one powerful tool is sufficient to cement a marriage into eternity. Respect will never disgrace, slander, cross, violate, or injure in any way.

When I think of the Fruit of the Spirit, I think of an orange, since it has slices within, representing love, joy, and longsuffering. While love is only one segment of the Fruit, it is enough to permeate the other sections. After all, the new Commandment given to us by Jesus is to love.

No born-again Christian has any reason not to display love to the world, because God's *agape* love has been imparted into their spirit at the time of salvation. Romans 5:5 (KJV) reads, *". . . the love of God is shed abroad in our hearts by the Holy Ghost which is given unto us."* The love is there, but we must renew our minds daily so that our carnal thinking will begin to conform to the new man within (Romans 12:1-2). When we become new creatures in Christ Jesus, we are able to enjoy the in-pouring of God's Might into our spirits until we exude His Presence. *"And all people of the earth shall see that thou art called by the name of the Lord, and they shall be afraid of thee,"* (Deuteronomy 28:10 KJV). Once we begin to think as God wants us to, love for God's Creation will automatically be demonstrated.

Death Must Obey Us When We Walk In Love

When we walk in God's Love, even death must obey. One experience I had with raising the dead took place in front of a Christian bookstore in Gary, Indiana. I had just parked my car, and there was a tremendous crowd gathered in the street near the store. Naturally I was curious, and as I approached the crowd, one of the spectators informed me that they were waiting for the police and ambulance because a man was dead, having been hit by an automobile.

I politely pushed my way through the crowd and went directly to the unmoving body. "In the Name of Jesus, I command this man's spirit to return to his body!" At that very moment, the man's body leaped from the ground at least two feet or so, and the crowd went hysterical. I stayed long enough to see him sit upright.

Very quickly and unemotionally, I returned to my car, but before I could get there, several people grabbed my arm, trying to make me stay on the scene. My only response was, "My work is done." I completely forgot about the bookstore. When I returned to my car I drove around the corner, and just between you and me, I began to praise God with torrents of tears streaming from my eyes. God's Love in me was placed on display.

We must remember that it isn't ourselves who do the healing. We are mere vessels, sent to represent God. We are carriers of God's Anointing, and when we speak the Name of Jesus, demons must flee. Death has to depart when a child of God who walks in love comes on the scene and orders it to leave.

Our ultimate aim in this life should be to please Christ Jesus, and the new Commandment He gave us was to love. After all, He is the One who gave His precious Life for us all. We must begin to awaken the giants within us and do the work that God has called us to do. I recall reading *The Divine Exchange* by the late Derek Prince, one of the most respected Christian educators of our day. In his book, Mr. Prince makes plain the exchange Jesus made with us when He died at Calvary: He died so that we could live. He became poor so that we could become rich. He became sin so that we could become righteous, and so on. Such great power and authority, and most of all, Love, has been bestowed upon us who are members of His body. The same Spirit that raised Jesus from the dead lives inside our bodies, waiting for us to physically display God's living Word throughout the Earth.

> *"But if the Spirit of him that raised up Jesus from the dead dwell in you, he that raised up Christ from the dead shall also quicken your mortal bodies by his Spirit that dwelleth in you."*
>
> (Romans 8:11 KJV)

Christ Jesus is our head, and each of us who has become a Christian is a designated part of His body.

> *"So we, being many, are one body in Christ, and every one members one of another."*
>
> (Romans 12:5 KJV)

> *"Knowledge shall be increased."*
>
> (Daniel 12:4 KJV)

Time and again, either through Promises, demonstration, or simple enunciated verbiage, God reminds us that He wants to bless us as much as he has blessed some of His other generals of the faith (see Acts 10:34, Romans 2:11, and Colossians 3:25). There are contingencies for realizing the manifestation or fulfillment of God's Promises; nonetheless, the basic law implies that God is no respecter of persons. Carrying this principle a step further, just as God does not favor one person over the next, He does not favor one profession over another. Knowledge shall increase, God foretells. He does not simply mean that knowledge shall increase in the educational or academic field, or in the movie industry. The world is growing wiser in every capacity, from garbage incinerator to garbage disposal to garbage disintegrating, and in the transformation of structural engineering, which has become advanced enough to build man-made islands in the middle of the ocean. We watch sheep being cloned, making an exact live replica, and bridges being built in a matter of weeks. The full spectrum of the world's diversity is enjoying increased knowledge.

But while knowledge is increasing, the love of many has waxed cold. This is the day when the love of money has surfaced to a degree that we could not imagine some twenty-five years ago. There was a saying when I was a kid: "Soap is a nickel, water is free; come on baby, take a bath with me." That was our candid, unrefined way of telling a playmate he had a body odor. No longer can we sing that song, because the cost of a small bottle of water, in some elite places, has soared to $3 a bottle, maybe more. That, of course, would be water *highly concentrated with minerals*. The Bible tells me that the Earth itself stands on a bed of water:

> *The earth is the LORD's, and the fullness thereof; the world, and they that dwell therein. For he hath founded it upon the seas, and established it upon the floods."*
> (Psalm 24:1-2 KJV)

Stop and imagine this world, with all its buildings, mountains, bridges, people, trains, ranches, and everything else we can possibly imagine, standing on the floods, the waters. This is just another example of our inability to fathom God, our Creator.

All water originates underground, and our soil is filled with nutrients, especially minerals. Mind you, the two major minerals in the body are calcium and magnesium. All minerals are formed underneath the ground. If the water comes from the same source as minerals, it must be loaded with minerals — at least, that's how I see it, via simple deductive reasoning. But it's the world's system. Marketing is a trigger-blasting, endless cycle of etymological and euphemistical harmonization. It's the harmony, not the reasoning, that sends folks flying to the markets to make purchases. On the contrary, there's nothing new under the sun. In the days of Moses, they were purchasing water.

Simultaneously, while we are experiencing an increase in the love of money, the Bible predicts that lawlessness will increase. *"And because iniquity shall abound, the love of many shall wax cold,"* (Matthew 24:12 KJV). This is certainly a time when the world calls right wrong and wrong right.

As a new convert, I experienced a joy that could never be explained. I had a love so open and pure that I told everyone I met about Christ and His precious Love for them. As for the church, I just knew that all Christians felt the way I was feeling. I found myself in church one Sunday, not long after my conversion, beautifully dressed in my perfect-fitting red wool suit, size 8, with an elegant white blouse. The Holy Spirit was flowing, and so was I, as I sat next to a gentleman who was quite visible in the community. I didn't know him on a personal basis, only through speaking at gatherings. At one point the pastor asked the congregation to join hands. Boy, did I hold his hand. I felt such love in my heart that I not only wanted to hold his hand, but also I wanted to hug him with a heavenly embrace. I didn't do the hug thing, though, but my hand-hold was so intense that it was mistaken for a sensual pass. I received the shock of my life when this gentleman snatched his hand from mine, stared at me with dagger blades streaming from his eyes, and moved away. I was so hurt that I nearly cried. I thought all Christians felt the love I was enjoying. I assumed that my new life was real to everyone professing Christ as Savior. Oh, how I wish it would be, both then and now.

The most perilous adversary to your spiritual progression is to permit your love to wax cold. However, God is Love. God does not have love; God *is* Love.

Only recently, while viewing the Sid Roth Show, I got the full revelation of the true meaning of God's Love for us. There was a guest on Sid's show who had died and gone to Heaven. When Sid asked him to describe Jesus, the guest stated that the only possible way he could describe Jesus was "Love". But, he didn't stop there.

This guest said that when he looked at Jesus' hands, he saw and felt Love. When he looked at Jesus' feet, eyes, and every other part of His body, he was infused with Jesus' endless Love. This guest said that Jesus had so much Love for him that He made him feel as though he was the only person in the entire world, and all of Jesus' Love was for him and him alone. Imagine, because *we* are the bride of Christ, all of His Love is for each of us only.

Jesus *is* love, and because we are in Jesus, God wants us to exemplify Him in every way. That means we should practice love with every grain of our intention, so intensely that it emanates from the core of our very being.

I want that love so earnestly. For the past few days, I've been talking to my body parts: "Eyes, you are love. You will see only through God's Eyes from this day forth. Hands, you are love. When you touch God's Creation, the love of God will pour through you. Feet, you are love," and so forth.

What Real Love Does, An Australian's Experience

I am reminded of a true story of an Australian evangelist who exuded God's love. There was a home for unwanted and abandoned children in a little town, which he had discovered and was determined to visit. The children were unwanted because their little bodies had been birthed with deformities, and their parents were not mentally, morally, spiritually, or socially equipped to challenge society or satan. Some were even convinced by the world's system that if they put the child in an institution, it would relieve them of social embarrassment and life could go on as usual. The children's lives had been labeled worthless.

But the Love of God infiltrated every inch of this evangelist's body, and he wanted to visit this facility, knowing that God would meet him there. Psalms 62:5 admonishes us, *"My soul, wait [look for help] thou only upon God; for my expectation is from him."*

God responds to our faith, and He met the evangelist there, just as expected. One by one, room by room, this gentleman visited the children, and he would lift the little babies' frail, fragmented bodies up in his arms. As he lifted these children up, he never saw their deformities or disabilities, only the Love of God in their eyes and hearts. The power of love was so overwhelming that each little body cracked, whipped, and jerked itself into place. Arms and fingers were straightened, legs unraveled, and eyes uncrossed. Doctors had pronounced the children vegetables, but God had a different prognosis. That little town enjoyed a revival that it had never dreamed possible.

> *"For what if some did not believe? Shall their unbelief make the faith of God without effect? God forbid, yea, let God be true, but every man a liar; as it is written That thou mightest be justified in thy sayings, and mightest overcome when thou art judged."*
>
> (Romans 3:3-4 KJV)

For those who are helpless, God will send them strength through one of His vessels who expects Him to perform according to His Word. Moreover, for those of us who are well able to think, look, seek, and ask for ourselves, God expects us to *expect* Him to perform on our behalf.

> *"For I know the thoughts that I think toward you, saith the LORD, thoughts of peace, and not of evil, to give you an expected end."*
>
> (Jeremiah 29:11 KJV)

God's Thoughts are so much higher than ours, and He so deeply desires that His children prosper and be in health as we grow in the revelation of Him.

This brave Australian evangelist brought Heaven to Earth. He demonstrated that God's Word is Life, and every Word written therein is positive and final. This Australian gentleman had such a repository of love stashed inside of him that when he held those deformed babies in his arms, their bones straightened out. All abnormalities on the babies' bodies were healed by love.

Be Careful How You Entertain Strangers At Church

I was in the church, a place where I thought the Love of God was manufactured, processed, and distributed, and yet, as a brand new saint, when attempting to extend my love, I was rejected. What does this tell us? Christians go to church but find themselves defensive. The love they have is for themselves, not for sharing.

> *"A new commandment I give unto you, That ye love one another; as I have loved you, that ye also love one another."*
>
> (John 13:34 KJV)

Loving one another is a command from the Commander in Chief, so it isn't just loving money, which may cause a fatal threat to our Christian walk. Sadly, our love for each other sometimes waxes cold. In one of his messages, Bill Johnson, one of the most prolific teachers of God's Word today, stated the following regarding Christians going to church: "You can wind up having a right religion about church doctrines while living a life without Christ. And, the sad thing is, you don't even know the difference."

Someone, somewhere had the right idea. Along the U.S. Interstate Highway between Jacksonville, FL, and East Chicago, IN, a sign was posted on a huge billboard: "You know that 'love your neighbor' thing? I meant that. Signed, God." I applaud the ingenious craftiness of the author. How can we say we love God, whom we have never seen, and then turn around and despise our neighbor? God says if we say we love Him and do not love those whom we see and walk with daily, we are liars and there is no truth in us. What God says, He means, and it's time His children realized the validity of His written Word and begin practicing it with sincerity so that our inheritance evolves from spiritual to experiential. God's Promises can only become ours to enjoy when we pull the Words from the pages with our mouth, lifestyle, and confidence to know that the Promises are true.

Love is more powerful than the universe because Heaven and Earth shall pass away, but love never fails. Love has no boundaries and is infinite in length, height, width, and depth. I think 1 Corinthians 13 gives us only a trace of what genuine love is, because God *is* Love, and He cannot be conveyed through mere words. Love suffers long and is kind; it does not envy or boast or puff itself up. Love does not behave in an unseemly way; it is not selfish, easily provoked, or evil. Love never fails.

IT'S TIME HIS CHILDREN REALIZED THE VALIDITY OF HIS WRITTEN WORD AND BEGIN PRACTICING IT WITH SINCERITY SO THAT OUR INHERITANCE EVOLVES FROM SPIRITUAL TO EXPERIENTIAL.

Chapter Fourteen

REFUSE TO LIVE WITH PRIDE

"Pride goes before destruction, And a haughty spirit before a fall."

(Proverbs 16:18 NKJV)

P ride will probably block a healing quicker than any other sin, because it will cause you to deny that you are in need of help from One greater than yourself.

"And they came to Jericho and as he went out of Jericho with his disciples and a great number of people, blind Bartimaeus, the son of Timaeus, sat by the highway side begging. And when he heard that it was Jesus of Nazareth, he began to cry out, and say, Jesus, thou son of David, have mercy on me. And many charged him that he should hold his peace; but he cried the more a great deal, Thou son of David, have mercy on me. And Jesus stood still, and commanded him to be called, And they called the blind man, saying unto him, 'Be of good comfort, rise; he calleth thee.' And he casting away his garment, rose, and came to Jesus. And Jesus answered and said unto him, 'What wilt thou that I should do unto thee?' The blind man said unto him, Lord, that I might receive my sight. And Jesus said unto him, Go thy way; thy faith has made thee whole. And immediately he received his sight, and followed Jesus in the way."

(Mark 10:46-52 KJV)

Bartimaeus was blind, and then Jesus healed him. Why? Because of his faith. When he was in the crowd amonsgt the arrogant religious group and the most hostile people in town, they pushed him back and trampled over him, hollering back, ["Shut up! Can't you see that Jesus is busy, and He has more important people to heal. We'll be back to give you a bite."

Ludicrous, blind Bartimaeus must have thought, and he kept calling Jesus, louder and louder. My first reaction was, how in the world are you going to convince a beggar, one who begs as a profession, to stop begging? Here is a man who makes his living seeking help. Here is a man who has daily thrown himself at the mercy of the general public and sustains himself by the public's response. How much more will blind Bartimaeus pursue help from One whom he had heard, trusted, and believed could heal him and give him sight, One who never fails, could supply his every need, open blind eyes, and cause the blind to see? Bartimaeus disregarded public opinions, put his faith into action, and demonstrated to Jesus that he was worthy of His Mercy. And Jesus rewarded him.

One of the greatest saints of our day, who proliferates God's healing powers, is Gloria Copeland. In her book, *Blessed Beyond Measure*, she writes:

> "What Bartimaeus did next was one of the most beautiful expressions of faith recorded in the New Testament. He threw off his cloak. History reveals that action had special significance,[" (pp 167, 168). One commentary says, "The cloak (Mark 10:50) is an outer garment, used as a coat in cold weather and as bedding at night, and might have been spread before him for use in his daytime begging if he had no pouch. The act of casting it aside may signify his forsaking dependence on anything else and trusting only in Jesus," says C. S. Keener (The IVP Bible background commentary: New

Testament, Mark 10:49-11:1)."I firmly believe that when Bartimaeus threw off his cloak, he was never planning to use it as a begging pouch again. By that act, he was making a very clear statement. He was saying, 'I'm not a blind man anymore. Jesus has heard me, and I'm as good as healed.'"

This was blind Bartimaeus' opportunity. Jesus hadn't passed this way before, and He may never pass this way again. He wasn't going to miss this once in a lifetime opportunity to receive his sight. A spirit of pride must have attempted to take a hold on him, but he rebuked it, "Have mercy on me!" In other words, "I need help! I can't do it alone! There's no other person living who can help me! You have the power to heal me, and I beg for Your mercy!" He cried out louder than he had ever cried before.

Crying out to God is important, children of God. Just as it is with salvation, many reading this book will recall that when the pastor or minister called for you to come forth to receive Jesus as Savior, you were embarrassed because you did not want the others watching you. That's a demon of pride. He worked on most of us that way, and I'm sure he whispered in blind Bartimaeus' ear, never thinking of his profession. Bartimaeus pushed through that spirit as I am certain many of you did when you walked forward. Oftentimes, our pride will shield our mouths, too, keeping us from letting go and earnestly beseeching God for His Blessings. Now that the devil is being exposed, do as blind Bartimaeus did: Scream louder!

I Believe God Saved Me From Lung Cancer

On a different subject, but equally important: To illustrate the cry of the heart, during the time I was a new convert, I smoked Kool cigarettes until smoke rose from my nostrils. I was on fire for God and never missed an opportunity to preach Jesus. About four months into my newly-converted life, my girlfriend and I were on our way back to my house when we met a stranger on the street. He was a very ripe catch for conversion, and I invited him to join us. I had a lovely home, and I knew that it would be a great tool for ministry. I used it as a bait, and it had worked several times before. I fed the young man a ham sandwich and Pepsi (a definite no-no today), then I sat down at the dining room table and read him Scripture after Scripture on salvation. After he left, my girlfriend reprimanded me, "You make the sorriest witness for God I've ever seen in my life."

I was shocked, "What do you mean?"

"I mean that cigarette. The whole time you were witnessing to that guy, you were blowing smoke in his face."

Immediately, I took a defensive posture, "What Scripture says I can't smoke a cigarette?" She was the one who introduced me to Christ Jesus, and she knew about as much about the Bible as I did, which was very little. Neither of us knew 1 Corinthians 3:16-17 or 6:29 or Romans 14:7-8, all of which informs us that our bodies belong to the Lord. But God was not pleased, because a spirit of conviction overtook me. My entire body flushed.

I lived in Chicago back then, and it was winter. If you haven't been there, you've certainly heard about the winters in Chicago. I recall driving down the Dan Ryan Expressway when the weather was -10° F, and I would roll down my window when smoking so that the cigarette smoke would not leave a stench in the car. In addition, when I took a drag from the cigarette, I would bend down in the car so that no one driving down the highway would see me puffing. I would hide cigarettes in the house and deliberately forget where I tucked them. Later, when I ran out of cigarettes, I would go on a hunt until I found some.

I was an addict, and now I was under a deep conviction! I would purchase cigarettes, smoke one or two, feel guilty, and then throw away the rest of the pack. About two or three o'clock in the morning, I would put on my boots, slip on my mink coat over my pajamas, and go to the corner to purchase a pack of cigarettes. After the smoke, I would pray, "Lord, forgive me. I promise I'll never do it again." Then, one day, I was so tired of hiding and feeling convicted that I cried out to God, "Lord, I need help! I can't do this! Take the taste from me! Please, God!" I screamed, cried, snotted, and boo-hooed, and Heaven listened.

I lived in a condominium, and the elevator opened by the back door. Eighteen to twenty feet from the door was the dining room, and in the middle of the dining room sat the table, of course. The day after I had poured out my guts crying out to God, begging Him to help me to quit smoking, I got the shock of my life: I unlocked the side door leading to the dining room, walked toward the table, and dropped my purse on the chair. As I was opening my coat, I noticed *The Way* on the table. You may remember *The Way* which is a Bible translation called *The Living Bible*. It was the Bible my girlfriend had given to me the day I got saved, the same friend who told me what a terrible witness I was when she saw me smoking my cigarette while telling a lost soul about Jesus. She's the one, I believe, who prayed me through.

The Bible was lying open on the table, and out of the book came the words, *"IF YOU DO IT AGAIN, I'M GOING TO PUNISH YOU."* Yes, you read right! The words flowed out from the pages of the Bible into the shape of a huge horn or cornucopia, covering about six feet of the table and rising about two feet high. I have never been so terrified in my entire life! Right before my eyes, God's Word came alive!

When the Holy Spirit speaks to you, you know exactly what He's talking about; there isn't a shadow of a doubt. You do not have to second-guess Him, because He is the One residing inside of you who is doing the talking. Without thinking about it, I knew that God was warning me against smoking. He was warning me that if I smoked again, I would be punished.

232

All I remember after that is slamming the book shut and falling to the floor as my knees went limp and buckled underneath my body. I cried and cried, pleading with God to forgive me.

The next day, as I passed the cigarette store, my flesh crawled and screamed for a smoke, but I was so afraid of God's punishment that I was wise enough not to entertain the cry of the flesh. 1 Corinthians 10:13 (KJV) came alive in my spirit: *"There hath no temptation taken you but such as is common to man: but God is faithful, who will not suffer you to be tempted above that ye are able; but will with the temptation also make a way to escape, that ye may be able to bear it."* I had not memorized the entire Scripture, but I knew enough to say that I would not be tempted. I knew that just as Jesus had commanded satan to get behind Him, I could, and I did. I was at war, and since the Commander in Chief had spoken, I had won. My love for God was far greater than my craving flesh. Moreover, I was utterly fearful of what might happen if I disobeyed God.

It has been decades since God delivered me from smoking, but I am thoroughly convinced that God saved me from satan, who was luring me into either lung or throat cancer. To any of you who have ever smoked, you understand how the body craves one cigarette after another. We understand better today that it is so difficult to quit smoking because it has been proven that cigarettes are being manufactured with additives to keep you addicted. Each time you inhale the cigarette smoke, you are increasing your risk of cancer.

Here is what the expert, Dr. Jonathan Foulds, states in his article, "Smoking and Lung Cancer":

> *"For some illnesses caused by smoking, smokers have a 50% or a 100% greater chance of getting that illness than never smokers. Stomach cancer and pneumonia are like that. A 100% greater risk doesn't mean 100% chance of getting the illness; it means double the chances of getting the illness as compared with the chances if you never*

smoked. For lung cancer, the increased risks are much greater. So a man who continues to smoke until he dies has 2300% increased risk of dieing [sic] of lung cancer: i.e., he is 23 times more likely to die of lung cancer, as compared with if he had never smoked." (http://www. healthline.com/health-blogs/freedom-smoking/ smoking-and-lung-cancer)

I had begged and pleaded for God to help me quit smoking, and God met me at a place where He knew I could respond. He knew if He rebuked me, that I loved Him enough to obey. God met me through the earnest cry of my heart. Countless times I prayed, asking Him to forgive me for smoking and promising never to do it again, only to surrender to the flesh. But, when the asking turned to fervently crying out to Him with sincere tears, He stepped in.

I have labored similarly in prayer on many occasions since that time, and whenever I reject the spirit of pride and let myself go, crying out to Him, He responds quickly. I am convinced that many are sick today because they do not cry out to God as blind Bartimaeus did. Just as it delighted Jesus to heal blind Bartimaeus, it delights Him to see you healed. Bartimaeus deliberately positioned himself to come into Jesus' presence. God wants us to seek Him like a thirsty deer, finally finding that stream of water and lapping it up, never able to quench the thirst, wanting the entire brook, and then realizing that it's more than the body can hold.

> *"As the deer pants for the water brooks, So pants my soul for You, O God."*
>
> (Psalm 42:1 NKJV)

Chapter Fifteen

HOW TO RECEIVE YOUR HEALING

"... And in all your getting, get understanding."
(Proverbs 4:7 NKJV)

Healing already belongs to you, through your redemption in Christ Jesus, but you must understand how easy it is for you to accept and enjoy it.

First, you must know that God's Promises are true. Every Word of God is 'yes', and that's final.

"Forever O Lord, thy word is settled in heaven."
(Psalm 119:89 KJV)

"For all the promises of God in him are yea, and in him Amen, unto the glory of God by us."
(2 Corinthians 1:20 KJV)

The Greek word for 'salvation' in the Bible is *soteria* [pronounced so-teri-a], and it means complete and total deliverance and success here on this Earth, including healing. Just as we must know the reality of God's Word and what it promises about being born again and being made new Creations in Christ Jesus, we must know and have faith to receive what God's Word promises about health and healing.

Second, we must know that as God's children we are members of the Royal family. When we understand that God is literally our Father, and it is a true Father's role to provide for, cultivate, and protect His children, it becomes easy for us to receive the healing that God has provided for us through the precious, atoning Blood

235

of Christ Jesus. God wants His children to depend only on Him, even for healing. That doesn't mean we exclude doctors, but God wants us to consult Him regarding the doctor. Is your doctor saved? He or she had better be, because God wants to instruct the doctors regarding your treatment. Remember: What does light have to do with darkness?

Third, as a child of God, you must know that it is your Father's Will for you to enjoy His best, which is walking in divine health. In the event that you become ill, know that healing has already been provided for you through the Blood of Jesus. Simply receive your healing with childlike faith. It is so much your Father's Will for you to walk in divine health that He made every provision in His written Will called the New Testament.

> *"For where a testament is, there must also of necessity be the death of the testator. For a testament is of force after men are dead; otherwise it is of no strength at all while the testator lives."*
>
> (Hebrews 9:16-17 KJV)

Our testator, Jesus Christ, died and gave His life so that you could receive this Will. After reading it, take your inheritance, child of God.

Fourth, pray God's healing Promises over your body three times daily, reminding Him of His Promises (Isaiah 43:26).

Finally, see yourself healed! Praise and worship God for what He has given you, sharing your blessings with someone else. (Rev 12:11)

Keeping Your Healing

Never accept an adverse report concerning your physical or mental condition. The moment you pray in faith, God hears and answers your prayer (Daniel 10:12). Many times, there is a delay in the manifestation, but faint not because angels are working on your behalf to see that your healing is manifested. Your responsibility is to continue thanking God for His Promises to heal you. God says in Exodus 23:25-26 that He took sickness from the midst of you, and you *must* trust His Promises. In Proverbs 4:20-23, He has promised that His Word is health to all your flesh, so we *must* continue inclining our ear to His Word. Any healing Scripture you remind God of will become your very own, provided you speak it continually and with gratitude.

If you have asked God to heal you, then your healing has begun; simply wait for its manifestation. The angels of God transport your words to God, and God in turn begins to administer health to your flesh (Daniel 10). Matthew 8:17 tells us that Christ Jesus healed all manner of sickness and disease through His precious Blood. After praying for your healing, you must accept, based on faith in God's Word, that it's already done. It's up to you to keep your healing. I've prayed for hundreds of people, and when they left me, in the majority of cases, I never saw what happened, but I believed my prayers worked. Sure enough, days, weeks, months, and even years later, a few of those for whom I had prayed drifted back, one by one, giving me reports of how God healed them. Your job is to pray; God does the rest!

Do not consider what you see with your physical eyes. You must be fully persuaded that what God has promised He is able to perform. Read Romans 4, the story of Abraham and Sarah, who relied on God's Promises even though they were well up in age and their bodies barren. Never consider what you feel, because faith is not a feeling. Simply stand on God's Word, trusting what He promises. This is what we call 'childlike faith', which never waivers. Never speak negatively about your healing; only say what God says. This is important. I believe another word for 'faith' is simply the Word of God. Faith only says what God says.

Do Not Allow The Sickness To Return

Once you have been prayed for, healing is yours. Keep praising God. If the devil attempts to bring back the symptom, such as a pain, rebuke it at once. Say what Jesus said to satan: *"Get thee behind me, satan."* Or you may simply say, "I bind you, pain, and command you, invading demon, to leave my body in the Name of Jesus. I praise and thank You, Father, for healing me." God has given you the power, so use it! Call the symptom by name, and the demons must leave at the Name of Jesus. It is so simple and it works every time.

A Few More Healing Scriptures

Get a revelation from any of the following healing Scriptures, whichever one(s) you favor, and begin to make them personal. Speak them out loud at least three times daily. God honors your confession (Romans 10:9-10). Or, it may very well be that you have your own favorite healing Scriptures.

- God wants us to turn to Him in repentance and have faith in the Lord Jesus Christ. (Acts 20:21)
- God wants us to bless Him for all of His benefits, including our healing. (Psalm 103:1-5)
- God promises that you will not die, but live to tell of His wonderful works. (Psalm 118:17)
- God promises to sustain you while on your sickbed and restore you to health. (Psalm 41:3)
- God promises to heal you so that you can enjoy His Kingdom. (Luke 10:9)
- *"This sickness is not unto death, but for the glory of God, that the Son of God might be glorified thereby."* (John 11:4 KJV)

- Just as Jesus healed the sick and cured the people of their diseases, He is doing the same for you because He is no respecter of persons. (Luke 7:2)

- Christ Jesus has compassion on you and is healing you right now. (Matthew 15:13)

- As you meditate on God's Word, you prosper and your health springs forth. (3 John 2)

- *"You are freed from your sickness."* (Luke 13:12 NASB)

- God has compassion for you. (Isaiah 49:13)

- The atoning Blood of Christ Jesus has healed you. (Isaiah 53:4-5)

- God's Word is alive and seeps into the marrow of your bones, bringing health. (Hebrews 4:12)

- God has taken sickness away from you. (Exodus 23:25-26)

- Just as Jesus healed the multitude, He's healing you as you go to Him. (Matthew 15:30)

- *"Your faith has made you well; go in peace and be healed of your affliction."* (Mark 5:34 NASB)

- God has compassion and will strengthen you. (Zechariah 10:6)

- God's Word is life and health to your body. (Proverbs 4:20-22)

- Jesus is living in you and gives life to your body. (Romans 8:11)

- *"Heal me, O LORD, and I shall be healed; save me, and I shall be saved: for thou art my praise."* (Jeremiah 17:14 KJV)

- Jesus will take up your infirmities and heal your diseases. (Matthew 8:16-17)

- Your body is a temple to the Holy Spirit. (1 Corinthians 6:19-20)

- God sends forth His Word and heals. (Psalm 107:20)

The Choice is Yours: Stay Well or Get Healed

Which is better for you, to remain well or to get healed? The question is really a no-brainer. If you are in perfect health today, stay that way! Congratulations is in order for all of you who choose to STAY WELL!

On the other hand, if you are not well and require a healing in your body, by all means, GET HEALED! Simply follow God's guidelines presented here before you and watch how quickly sickness leaves your body.

No one enjoys being sick, not even the misinformed religious community which is convinced that God wants them that way so that they can glorify Him. How, tell me, does sin compliment glory? After all, sickness is sin, and Jesus was crucified for every sin imaginable.

> *"But He was wounded for our transgressions, He was bruised for our iniquities; the chastisement of our peace was upon Him, And by His stripes we are healed."*
> (Isaiah 53:5 NKJV)

The very God who gave His only begotten Son to die for our sins, the God who is Creator of all the universe, certainly does not need nor would He settle for any of satan's tactics to debilitate, demote, distress, or disgrace His children in any way. Nor does He require or use any of satan's tactics to elevate His children. The thief comes to steal, kill, and destroy, and sickness does all three:

(1) Sickness steals. There is no sudden attack; it enters the body little by little, as with food. You eat porkchops, fried chicken, French fries, hamburgers, cookies, cake, and candy day in and day out, enjoying it more and more until you

become addicted. While your flesh is gulping down these inhibitors of a long life, the carcinogens they produce are wreaking havoc through the cells in your body, pouring in toxins and destroying your cardiovascular system by plugging up your arteries with plaque via hydrogenation. Did you know that hydrogenated oils were originally developed to produce low-cost soap? They are artificially developed by converting liquid fats into solids, such as lard, non-dairy cream, margarines, bakery products, and nut butters. Then comes sickness. And you thought it happened all of a sudden. No, it started the moment you deviated from God's dietary plans for your life. The thief has invaded your body because all of the symptoms go unnoticed.

(2) Sickness kills not just the body but also the mind and soul. Your thoughts are foggy and you have a decrease in memory because your brain cells are dying. Your mobility is not what it was when you were twenty-five. You have listened to distorted messages from satan, that when you get older, you automatically slow down and your mind fades away.

(3) Sickness destroys everything about you. Nothing works in harmony anymore. You are at a place where you feel death is better than life.

In all sincerity, no one truly believes that God wants them to be sick, because if they truly believed that farce, they would not go to the doctor or use any other measures to get healed. They would praise God every time a pain struck them and pray continually for more pain and sickness, if they truly believed that their sickness glorified God.

We have exposed satan and his many tricks for causing sickness in our bodies. The fact is, according to God's Word, we do not have to get sick. I have repeated God's prescription for healing in Ezekiel 47:12: fruit for meat, leaves for medicine. The world's top medical physicians could not make the prescription plainer in any language. We also shared Genesis 1:29, where God prescribed the herbs for meat. So we have two different kinds of meat, fruits and herbs, by God's prescriptions.

As I mentioned, *The Hallelujah Diet* by Dr. George Malkmus is probably the best diet to take us back to the Garden of Eden and restore our health. Following his plan is sure to cause you to rediscover your youth. You may want to contact his office. Dr. Don Colbert's book, *What Would Jesus Eat,* steers us to a great Mediterranean diet. Why not purchase these books as a part of your pledge to begin a new lifestyle?

One of the best foods on 'God's Green Earth' is celery. I believe that a person with high blood pressure will find that the symptoms will disappear within six to eight weeks when eating at least half an entire stalk of celery a day. I use a blender and place about half a cup of crushed ice in the bottom, chop the celery into two-inch chunks, and toss the chunks into the blender. I add a scoop each of vegetable protein and powdered rice milk or half a cup of almond milk. I add two or three tablespoons of walnuts, almonds, pecans, and a handful of whatever fruit I have in the refrigerator (Blueberries and blackberries are my favorites.). I usually add spinach, asparagus, kale, or any other raw vegetable in season, and blend. This makes the most delicious raw food smoothie you ever want to drink — a delicious glass filled with healing foods.

Nutrients are a must. It is unreasonable today, with so much contaminants in our soils and pollutants in our foods, to think that you do not need nutrients. I cannot overemphasize the importance of taking high-quality nutrients.

My daily regime includes:

- Whole-food multivitamin with enzymes
- Pure deep-water fish oil, high in DHA
- Vitamin E, 1000 IU
- Garlic
- Multi-mineral
- CoQ10, 400 mg
- Vitamin B12, 5000 mcg
- Life's Wonder MCHA Calcium & Magnesium
- Vitamin B complex, 100 mg
- L-Carnitine, 3000 mg
- Pycnogenol or grapeseed, 100 mg
- Vitamin C, 3000 to 5000 mg
- Vitamin D$_3$

For preventative measures, I take milk thistle and dandelion periodically for my liver and kidneys, glucosamine sulfate and collagen for the joints. I frequently take a quality eye nutrient. I regularly take strong doses of Alpha Lipoic Acid to protect the nerve sheaths throughout my body, as all diabetics should according to Dr. Balch. Other nutrients I take are hit and miss, based on what I feel I may need from time to time, but never a day passes that I do not add very special nutrients for isolated areas of my body.

Most of you who are reading this book have committed your life to Christ, which means that you believe that Christ Jesus gave His Life in order that your sins would be forgiven and that you would not have to suffer sickness. It is my sincere prayer that you begin to practice what you believe.

Chapter Sixteen

STAY IN THE GLORY REALM

There is a place where divine health dwells; its beauty and brilliance far outweigh man's ability to capture with words the greatness of its splendor. It is located in a room called the Sanctuary or Throne Room, and the King of Glory sits there bidding you to come. In the Glory Realm rests the Presence of God, and though accessible, few will find the time or discipline to go there. The Glory Realm is a place where flesh and foolishness are forbidden, opinions and oppressions cannot enter, and decisions can never be made there. It is a place where the submissive heart yields to His Will.

It is a very private place, where guests are forbidden. The Master Himself awaits you as you enter the door, for He has reserved His Glory just for you and no one else. God and you — you and God. That's all. Nothing and no one else is needed, nor can they be accepted, no, no, not at this time, and not in this very special place. It is a secret place, because no one knows that you are there except you and Him. Nice, huh?

So, come on in. Simply still yourself and prepare for another encounter with eternity. Many things happen in the Realm of Glory, and they are all huge! This is the place where you cannot miss receiving your healing. Why? Because you are now completely in Him and He is in you, and where He is, sin cannot come. Sickness is sin, and all that He paid for has been redeemed. That means you. There are no credits or returns in this realm. SO, COME IN. YOU ARE HEALED!

Endnotes

1   www.thinkbabynames.com   The boy's name Simon \s(i)-mon\ is pronounced SYE-mun. It is of Hebrew origin, and the meaning of Simon is "to hear, to be heard; reputation". Biblical: Simon was the name of two of the apostles, including Simon Peter. A common name from the Middle Ages through the 18th century. Orchestra conductor Simon Rattle; Latin American freedom fighter Simon Bolivar.

2   www.chacha.com

3   Deuteronomy 34:7 And Moses was an hundred and twenty years old when he died: his eye was not dim, nor his natural force abated.

4   Mark 6:31 And he said unto them, Come ye yourselves apart into a desert place, and rest a while: for there were many coming and going, and they had no leisure so much as to eat.

For questions or comments please contact us at:

Tricked Into Sickness
Post Office Box 26428
Jacksonville, FL 32226
www.trickedintosickness.net
e-mail: trickedintosickness@gmail.com

CPSIA information can be obtained
at www.ICGtesting.com
Printed in the USA
FFOW03n1255040618
47060680-49409FF